365 Sales Tips for Winning Business
based on the popular 1997 calendar of the same name, selected by Sales & Marketing Management Magazine *as one of its "Hot Gifts" for that year.*

Here's what users of the calendar said about Tips:

"Only five to ten seconds of reading and it speaks volumes. My best buddy!"

—JOHN BASISTA, sales rep
Novartis Pharmaceuticals
Youngstown, OH

"A real short, concise, and useful tool. Fun and practical!"

—ED BUTTS, sales manager
Diamond Crystal Specialty Foods
Melrose, MA

"An easy reference and reminder for sound business and sales techniques. We tend to forget the basics and the calendar kept us on track."

—TONY SCATURRO, AVP Worldwide
Customer Service/Sales Operations
NCR
Dayton, OH

"I gave *365 Sales Tips* calendars to the entire sales and marketing departments as holiday gifts last year. [The tips] paid daily dividends in increased sales and profitability."

—BOB SCHUBERT, vice president, Sales & Marketing
Sermatech International
Limerick, PA

"One of my reps made a $2,000 commission with just one of the Closing tips. This calendar was one of the best investments I ever made for the staff."

—VIGGIO MADSEN, director, National Sales
Dentrix Dental Systems
American Fork, UT

"I love it! Every time I need a little lift, I find just the right quote. I also pass the quotes around to my staff."

—JENNIFER SAIA, president/charter specialist
Sacks Yacht Charters
Ft Lauderdale, FL

"It's like a one-a-day vitamin pill that gives salespeople energy for the whole day!"

—JOHN C. TRAVERS, president
Data Arts & Sciences
Natick, MA

"We send out *Tips* on broadcast messages to our branches. Associates use the tips and e-mail the results. Best of all, they send in their own sales tips for broadcast."

—JUDY SOCCIO, editor, Retail Sales & Marketing
Mellon Bank
Pittsburgh, PA

"Made my salespeople more aware of the daily thoughts, skills and reactions that make or break a sale. These tips are tops!"

—WANDA DESHAY, supervisor, Sales
National Data Corporation
Hanover, MD

"Excellent Christmas gifts for my sales force. So many of the tips were put to use throughout the year. Our sales have increased 127 percent."

—RICH GIELOW, manager, Regional Sales
Wilson Sporting Goods Co.
Orangevale, CA

"Keeps a tip-a-day top of mind, which gets reinforced all day, day after day. Really helpful!"

—THAD RIEDER, manager, Sales & Marketing
Lindberg/MPH (Div. General Signal Corp)
Riverside, MI

"I only wish there were 400 days in the year. Keep those tips coming!"

—STEPHEN J. SCHWARTZ, vice president/associate publisher
Chemical Week
New York, NY

"I really enjoyed the calendar and have kept a lot of the tips. Absolutely helped me make money!"

—JOHN WESTRICK, manufacturer's rep
Environmental Protection Coatings
Bradenton, FL

"Tips calendar assisted my team in two ways. First, it kept us thinking sales every day! Secondly, your tips helped us revisit sales scenarios that had made us successful in the past. I personally used your calendar because I enjoyed it!"

—BILL BODEN,
Ecolab
Dayton, OH

Also by Anne Miller

PRESENTATION JAZZ! HOW TO MAKE SALES PRESENTATIONS $ING

365

Sales
Tips *for*
Winning Business

Anne Miller

A Perigee Book

A Perigee Book
Published by The Berkley Publishing Group
A member of Penguin Putnam Inc.
200 Madison Avenue
New York, NY 10016

Copyright © 1998 by Anne Miller
Book design by Tiffany Kukec
Cover design by Joe Lanni

First edition: August 1998

Published simultaneously in Canada.

The Penguin Putnam Inc. World Wide Web site address is
http://www.penguinputnam.com

Library of Congress Cataloging-in-Publication Data

Miller, Anne.
    365 sales tips for winning business / Anne Miller.—1st ed.
       p.   cm.
    "A Perigee book."
    ISBN 0-399-52419-3
    1. Selling.   2. Selling—Quotations, maxims, etc.   I. Title.
HF5438.25.M555   1998
658.85—dc21   98-5782
                                                          CIP

Printed in the United States of America

10   9   8   7   6   5   4   3   2   1

For
Helen & Leon,
Jay & Carol,
Matt & Dana

CONTENTS

Acknowledgments   xi
Introduction   xiii

PROBING   1

LISTENING   13

PRESENTING   23

HANDLING OBJECTIONS   39

CLOSING AND FOLLOW-THROUGH   55

NEGOTIATING   69

BUILDING RELATIONSHIPS   85

CREATIVE THINKING   97

WORKING SMART   107

ATTITUDE AND MOTIVATION   123

MEASURE YOUR SELLING POWER
    Personal Selling Power Profile   131

INDEX   135

ACKNOWLEDGMENTS

First and foremost, my thanks go to the thousands of clever, funny, and talented sales professionals I have been lucky enough to work with over the years. I never teach a seminar or give a speech when I don't learn a tip or two from them as well.

Additional warm thanks go to friends, fans, mentors, and clients, including: Annie Zehren, Cecile Rothschild, Sue Agresta, Janine Gordon, Richard Kinsler, Jim Fishman, Tom Evans, Bob Roth, Jim Donoghue, Jay Melvin, Larry Kaufman, Diane Cremin, Tom Larranaga, Susan Taylor, Debi Garner, Jerry Weiss, and Marshall Harrison. Deep appreciation to Alan Weiss for introducing me to my agent, Jeff Herman, who led me to John Duff, the terrific editor who helped get these ideas into tip-top shape.

INTRODUCTION

This book is a portable, personal sales coaching tool for busy salespeople who want to be the best in their business. It features thousands of dollars worth of practical, powerful, business-building ideas organized in ten critical success-skill categories: Probing, Listening, Presenting, Handling Objections, Closing and Follow-Through, Negotiating, Building Relationships, Creative Thinking, Working Smart, and Attitude and Motivation.

Are you worried about how to negotiate price in a big upcoming deal? Turn to the Negotiating Tips chapter and find your answer in tips 191, 197, and 206.

Are you having a bad day on the road, away from friends, colleagues, and family, and feeling down? Turn to the Attitude and Motivation chapter and renew yourself with motivational energy and advice.

Did you finally get that meeting with the senior decision-maker and are worried that your presentation might be just a little dry? Turn to the Presenting chapter and get quick ideas in tips 86, 87, and 89 for keeping your presentation interesting, persuasive, and memorable.

Each of the ten chapters in this book features specific tips, examples, and ideas to help you do your job more easily and effectively. These tips are based on the lessons I've learned over the past fifteen years, as a sales consultant, speaker, and seminar leader, working with hundreds and hundreds of salespeople all over the world.

Many Ways to Use This Book

This book is essentially a reference tool. Keep it with you at all times and consult it on an as-needed basis.

You can also use this book to assess your personal selling power. How many of these tips do you already know and are now using? Which ones are new, or refreshers, to you? As you read these tips, put a **check** in the box next to each tip you are now using. Put an **X** next to the tips that you are not using. Add the **checks** up for each section and write your score on the last page of each chapter. Transfer your scores from each chapter to the Personal Selling Power Profile on page 132 to determine your overall selling strength. Work on the tips you marked with an X to perfect your strongest selling skills and improve your weakest ones. You may even want to share the results of your self-assessment with your manager to help target his/her coaching with you.

Why not copy the tips you marked with a ✓ and post them where you are likely to see them every day? These will become **your** personal "Best Tips for Winning Business" reminders.

You can also use *365 Sales Tips for Winning Business*

with your whole sales team. Have each salesperson identify the best tips in any given section—a tip that has helped make money, save time, reduce stress, increase profits, etc. Then, at weekly sales meetings, spend fifteen minutes doing a "sales-tip-and-story swap." Each salesperson explains why he/she chose that particular tip and tells how it helped win business. Not only will this exercise reinforce the skills and strategies espoused in the tips, but this sharing of stories will also leverage the rich, collective success experiences of an entire staff.

Save everyone's favorite tips and have them typed up into one list. This list then becomes "Your Company's Best Tips for Winning Business." You can have these blown up to poster size with your logo on it and distribute the list to everyone to hang in their offices as constant reminders of the best things to do to win business.

Finally, have everyone on your staff write their favorite tips on individual pieces of folded-up paper. Put these papers in a large jar or box. Each week, a tip is fished out and that tip becomes the team's "Tip of the Week." It can be posted or e-mailed to everyone. Salespeople are reminded to use that tip in all appropriate circumstances as often as possible during that week. Results can be shared at a sales meeting or by interoffice correspondence (memos, e-mail).

If only one tip in this book works for you—gets you critical information, makes your presentations more persuasive, helps you close a deal, or gets you on your client's "A" list—then you've got your money's worth many times over. Start using these tips today. Make them your own and watch your business grow.

To share your selling tips, or, for further information on Anne Miller's sales and communications speeches, seminars, and audiotapes,

> call (212) 876-1875
> e-mail: amspeak@aol.com
> Visit my web site at www.chironassoc.com
> or, write:
> Anne Miller
> Chiron Associates, Inc.
> Box 624
> New York, NY 10163

PROBING

"When you think you've asked all the questions you can, ask one more!"

—CATHY VISCARDI,
Executive Vice President,
Conde Nast Publications

Questioning Mindset

☑ **1. See yourself as a combination doctor, consultant, and puzzle solver.** You're asking questions to figure out how you can best help this person *solve a problem or add value to an existing situation.* If you can do neither, you have nothing to sell.

☐ **2. "Sit" on the buyer's side of the table.** Do you see yourself across the table from your buyers in an adversarial role, trying to get limited dollars from them for your product, so you can make quota? Or, do you see yourself on the same side of the table in a partnership trying to solve their problems so that you both make money?

Somewhere in between? How you see your role drives how you will interact with clients.

❑ **3. Don't confuse the way you keep score with the process of selling.** Clients sense when you are interested more in making a sale than you are in helping them. Help clients get what they need (the *process* of selling) and you will earn what you want (the commissions or bonuses that you use to keep *score* of your sales performance.)

Preparation

✓❑ **4.** *"Chance favors the prepared mind."*

—LOUIS PASTEUR

Before you walk in, think through your call. What do you know about this account? What's your objective? How will you know you've achieved it? After you say hello, how will you move the dialogue forward?

✓❑ **5. Prepare questions in advance.** Jot down the key questions you want to ask your clients. This saves time on calls and guarantees that you won't miss any key information you needed to know.

✓❑ **6. People don't care how much you know until they know how much you care.** The first sign that you care is to demonstrate you took the time to do your homework on their business. For example, on a call to a software development company, instead of saying, "Tell me about your company," say, "I read that you're introducing a new customer tracking product for doctors. Tell me about that."

Early in the Conversation

☐ **7. Learn your customer's personal history.** In initial small talk with a prospect, or a new person on an existing account, find out his work history: where he was before, what brought him to this position or company. The buyer's responses often reveal how sophisticated he is about the business, his ambitions, his mandate, and/or his motivation.

☐ **8. Engage your buyer immediately.** Buyers decide pretty quickly whether a salesperson is worth their time. To make an immediate positive impression, focus your remarks on your buyer.

1. State your reason for the call, which is always to help the client.
2. Pique your buyer's interest. State two or three brief, appealing product facts to establish your credentials.
3. Set an agenda: "Let's review your situation, what my firm offers, and where there is a likely fit."
4. Check for agreement: "Is that okay?"

Now, the buyer knows the benefit of talking to you, how the time will be spent, and he's agreed to the agenda and to his participation. You're both on track for a meaningful dialogue.

☐ **9. Reconfirm time expectations.** Since you made your appointment, your buyer's time frames may have changed. It is always a good idea to double-check this early in the meeting.

☐ **10. Beware the early "Tell-Me-All-About-Your-Company" trap.** After an initial greeting, a buyer may ask you to tell him about your products or services. Without a fuller client discussion, it isn't clear what you should say that would be relevant.

1. Respond briefly: "We are a leader in the field. We work with firms of all sizes. In fact, we just finished a project for XYZ company in your industry."
2. Build a bridge to the buyer's world: "What we find is that every company is in a unique situation. For example, I read you are developing a new site in . . ."
3. Ask a question: "How is that going?"

☐ **11. Take notes.** It's hard enough to remember a shopping list of more than a few items. Don't trust your memory to be able to recall all the details of a sales conversation. Ask permission ("Do you mind if I take some notes?"), but take notes.

☐ **12. Four-quarter page notes.** Divide your page into four quarters. In one you put all notes relating to the facts of the *client's situation* and needs; in the second, notes about her *problems/challenges*; in the third, *objections and notes about your competition*; in the fourth, notes referring to *key people* in the decision-making process. You now have a document that will give you a summary of your discussion and a visual clue to what information is missing.

☐ **13. Bad notes.** Never write down any confidential or personal notes in front of buyers. They will immediately clam up if they see you recording sensitive information. Write down the juicy political and personal tidbits *after* you leave the office.

General Probing Guidelines

☐ **14. Spend the majority of discussion time on the buyer's business.** Verify your client's business facts: timing, objectives, specs, etc., quickly. Spend most of your time, 75 to 85 percent, discussing his problems or challenges in reaching his goals, the impact of these problems on the organization, the cost of doing nothing, the rewards for resolving these issues, and the options he's considered so far. This discussion will give you the key to making the most suitable recommendation for both you and your buyer.

❑ **15. Share information as you ask for information.** Instead of asking "How will your marketing strategy change this year?" say, "According to . . . , housing starts will jump 18 percent this year. How will this projected jump affect your plans?" If he knew about the jump, he thinks you're pretty sharp. If he didn't know about it, you just made him smart. Either way, you win.

❑ **16. Use cushions to ask tough questions.** Preface sensitive questions with nonforcing, easy lead-in phrases: e.g., "*Everyone is different in terms of how they make decisions.* What criteria will you be using?" "*No two companies are the same* in how they see. . . . What is your view of our product?" "*You know the situation best.* What will your budget be?" Cushions recognize the uniqueness of the buyer and are respectful of the individual. Most important, cushioned questions get answers.

❑ **17. Question like a camera.** Use *open* questions to get the wide-angle big picture. "How do you expect to use this product? What have you been doing up to now?" Use *closed* questions to zoom in on specifics. "Will you be starting in the next six months?" "Are you looking for 10,000 or 20,000 square feet of space?"

❑ **18. Create easy conversation.** The best probing or information-gathering discussion is a conversation, not an interrogation. The most powerful probing request is "Tell me more about that." Like a loose strand of wool that you gently pull until it's fully out of the sweater, this question encourages people to talk and, then, to talk some more.

☐ **19. Seed your discussion with success tidbits.** Before you are ready to offer a full-blown presentation or solution, drop hints of your firm's success into the conversation.

Buyer: "We want a plan that can accommodate the job-share needs of our female employees."

Seller: "*Oh, yes. You might know Jim Ryan down the street. He had a similar need, and we helped him with that.* What else will be important to you?"

Smart Questions

☐ **20. Use high-payoff questions.** High-payoff questions lead to a discussion. They get your buyer to reflect, to speculate, or to expand on a point. Example:

Buyer: "We don't feel that we need all these added features."

Weak:

Seller: "Why?"

Stronger:

Seller: "What is there about this project that leads you to that conclusion?"

◻ 21. Ask the $64,000 high-payoff question. People know their objectives, but they worry about the obstacles they face along the way. Your $64,000 question is, "What is the biggest problem or challenge facing you now?" You want to discuss with them why it's a problem and how it's impacting on their business. The key to your sale will be in addressing those problems.

◻ 22. Ask the "now" question. It is not enough to know that a buyer is in the market for a product or service. You want to understand why he is looking at this time. Asking "Why is this important to you (to the organization, to management) *now?*" reveals the source of the pressure to act.

◻ 23. Quantify the reward. Ask buyers what the *business value* is of solving their problems or reaching their goals. That value can be in revenues, profits, market share, cost savings, or some other measure. Whatever it is, by naming a number, buyers begin to see the advantages of taking action sooner rather than later.

◻ 24. Quantify the price of inaction. Ask buyers what the consequences of not solving their problems will be to the company, to key people in the company, to the bottom line, to the buyer personally. Whatever they are, by describing these negative consequences, buyers increase their motivation to act.

☐ **25. Quantify the time window.** Ask how long the company has to solve its problems. A month? A year? Longer? Defining the time pressure helps the buyer see the need for acting sooner rather than later.

☐ **26. Establish the buyer's stake in a solution.** Business needs are only half the picture. Find out what the buyer needs to "win" on a personal level as well. Is she new with a need to impress her boss? Has she been given a new mandate and limited time to make it happen? Does she want to pull this project off without making waves? Is she under pressure to come up with new ideas? Ask "What's important to you *personally* in this project?"

☐ **27. The budget question.** Instead of asking "What's your budget?" or "How much money do you have?" which can be confrontational or offensive, inquire "What financial resources will you be committing to this?" If the number is low, ask, "What led you to that number?" The buyer's answer will indicate how much of an obstacle price may be.

☐ **28. Find the players.** To determine the decision-making process, start to draw an organization chart. "Lisa, I know you are the AVP, Media, and Jeff is the media director." Then, pass the paper and pen to Lisa. "Can you tell me who else is involved in the decision-making process?" As she fills in the chart, ask key questions about each player.

Avoiding Assumptions

☐ **29. Be an explorer.** Before selling, explore the buyer's thinking. Ask: "What options are you looking at now to address this situation? Why?" The answers to these questions reveal total budget, the sophistication of the buyer's approach, and any additional benefits he is seeking.

☐ **30. Find out the client's "wish list".** Asking for his wish list will reveal the benefits he wants. Example: "If money were no object, what would be on your wish list? *Why?*" Or, "If you could wave a magic wand, what would you like to see in this product or service? *Why?*" You often cannot satisfy all the specs for a job, but you may be able to put together a package of alternatives that gives him the same benefits.

☐ **31. Will you be the right answer to the customer's needs?** Identifying the buyer's criteria is critical to your success. Ask "How will you know you have the right supplier (consultant, person) sitting in this chair?" This is an unusual way to ask for those criteria and it gets buyers to really think about what's important to them.

☐ **32. Test possible ideas/solutions.** Before you spill out all your wonderful features and benefits, test your buyer's thinking first.

Buyer: "We are targeting women in their late teens, early twenties."

Weak:

Seller: "Oh, you want to reach women in their late teens, early twenties? We can do that with this marvelous college program," blah, blah, blah.

Better:

"Oh, you want . . . early twenties? What thought have you given to reaching them when they're in college?"

The buyer's possible answers are none, interested, lots, rejected it, or we're already doing that. The buyer's response will indicate in what direction you will need to take this call.

☐ **33. Check buyer's perceptions.** Ask how the buyer views your product or service. Is he unfamiliar with it, harboring some concerns about it, or very positive about it? His response will indicate in what direction you will need to take this call.

☐ **34. Set up the next step in your probing discussion.** Sellers often feel pressure at the end of the call, when it comes time to close or move to the next step. Eliminate that problem. Establish the next step in the first half of the call.

Seller: "If we were, in fact, to work together, what would be our next step after today's meeting?"

Buyer: "You'd have to see Harry in MIS."

Assuming the call goes well, it becomes perfectly natural for you to say at the end of the meeting, "Great. I'll give Harry a call and then get back to you."

Buyer: "Fine."

☐ **35. Recap your discussion before selling.** When you think it's time to offer solutions or present your recommendations, summarize and check for accuracy first. "So, you want to accomplish . . . The challenges are . . . Time is critical. You're leaning toward using ABC and your concern about us would be the depth of our resources. Have I left anything out?"

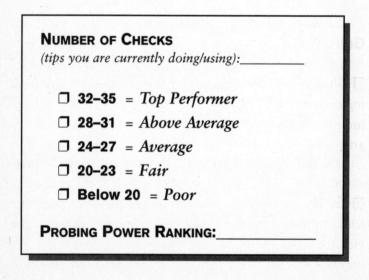

NUMBER OF CHECKS
*(tips you are currently doing/using):*_____

☐ **32–35** = *Top Performer*
☐ **28–31** = *Above Average*
☐ **24–27** = *Average*
☐ **20–23** = *Fair*
☐ **Below 20** = *Poor*

PROBING POWER RANKING:_____

LISTENING

"I . . . tell myself to listen . . . to be in their shoes when they talk; to try to know them without my mind pressing against theirs, or arguing, or changing the subject. No. My attitude is: 'Tell me more.'"

—BRENDA UELAND,
Strength to Your Sword Arm

General Guidelines

☐ **36. Hearing and listening are not the same.** Hearing means your ears are functioning. If a bell goes off, you jump because you hear it. Listening means you're paying attention. No one ever listened himself out of a sale.

☐ **37. Every buyer has the "right to be wrong."** Views, opinions, and preferences are based on each individual's perceptions and experiences. Listening and acknowledging these do not mean you endorse them.

❐ **38. Check your emotions and personal opinions at the door.** Focus on your *buyers'* views and opinions, however disagreeable they may be. Respectfully, ask for the reasons behind their statements. Only when you know their rationale can you hope to guide them to choosing your product or service.

❐ **39. Listen to everyone on an account.** Even disagreeable and dull customers have at least one good story in them, one piece of useful information to share, or one fresh perspective on a situation to give you.

❐ **40. Listen for cues that tell you how formal or informal to be.**

Seller (enthusiastically): "Hi! how are you?"
Buyer (politely): "Fine."
Seller thinks, "Whoa! This is going to be a lo-o-ong call!"

Not necessarily. All the client is saying by her cool response is that she needs more time to get to know the seller before being able to be that friendly. A good listener gauges what degree of informality is appropriate with a particular buyer.

❐ **41. Stick to your buyer's beat.** Everyone has a preferred speaking and thinking tempo. Some tempos are snappy and fast-paced. Others are more deliberate and slower paced. Follow your buyer's lead and pace yourself to her tempo.

☐ **42. Be "in the moment" with clients.** Sports pros concentrate on their game. They're not thinking of what it will be like to win. They're not thinking of past games. They are focussing on what is happening *now*! When you're with a client, clear your mind of personal distractions, thoughts of making quota, your next appointment, etc. Be there 100 percent.

☐ **43. Listen to learn and understand, not to speak.** When you are concentrating on what your response will be, then you aren't really listening—you are simply waiting your turn to talk. Buyers sense that immediately and shut down. You learn when you are listening, not when you are talking.

☐ **44. Look like a listener.** Sit up, look alert, lean forward.

Listening Skills

☐ **45. Be an encouraging listener.** Smile, nod, pay attention to buyers. Draw out their thinking with reactions like "Really!" "No kidding." "Tell me more." "And then?"

❐ **46. Let buyers talk.** Old saying: "We each have two ears and one mouth. We must therefore be meant to listen twice as much as we are meant to speak."

❐ **47. Let buyers finish their thoughts.** People who cut other people off in midsentence often cut their chances for building close client relationships at the same time.

❐ **48. Use different phrases for confirming what you think you're hearing.** Examples:

"So, you're saying you want to . . . ?"
"I'm hearing that you are primarily interested in . . . and
    not . . . Is that correct?"
"You're feeling that . . . Is that right?"
"My sense is . . . Is that right?"

❐ **49. Ask, ask, recap.** Summarizing periodically ensures that you have correctly heard what your buyer has said.

Seller: "What are you looking for in this position?"
Buyer: "I want someone with international experience,
    who has managed a division in the aerospace industry."
Seller: "Does it matter if the experience has been in Asia or
    in Europe?"
Buyer: "We prefer Asia."

Seller: "Okay. International experience, preferably Asia, with broad senior-level responsibilities. Right?"

Buyer: "Yes."

Seller: "What else will be important?"

❑ 50. Use a buyer's own word or phrase to sharpen weak listening skills.

Buyer: "I'm under pressure to have this done by July 1."

Seller: "Where is this *pressure* coming from?"

Buyer: "My boss thinks we should book these things at least six months in advance."

Seller: "What type of place is *your boss* looking for?"

❑ 51. Mirror, or echo, buyer's key word or issue.

Buyer: "I think this is going to be too risky."

Seller: *"Too risky?"*

Buyer: "Yes, we've never done anything like this before."

Seller: "So, it's not the product. Your concern is more about doing something new. Is that it?"

Buyer: "Yes, that's exactly what I mean."

❑ 52. Listen with your eyes as well as with your ears. Be alert to signs of impatience: buyer checking his watch, looking out the window, shifting in his chair, eyes glazing over. Respond to what you see. "Mr. Buyer, are we on track here?" "Are we discussing what you want to dis-

cuss?" "Is there something wrong?" There's no point in having a discussion if your buyer is not present in both body and spirit.

❐ 53. Listen for potential grenades. When you hear something that creates an emotional reaction in you, resist the (understandable) urge to strike back with a quick attack. Pause. Count to three. Then, confirm what you think you heard: "Am I correct that you're saying . . . ?" Next, ask: "What leads you to that view?"

❐ 54. Listen for contradictions. Don't let mixed messages mix you up.

Buyer: "Our supplier relationship is solid."
(Ten minutes later.) Buyer: "We're talking to New Supplier X about changing the heating system."
Seller: "*Could we clarify something you said earlier?* On the one hand, you said you're set with your supplier. Now, you seem to be suggesting that you are seeking new ones. Does this mean that you are, in fact, open to other bids on this project?"

❐ 55. Listen for what you don't understand. Clarify the unfamiliar. "Sue, I'm sorry, but FSG is a term that is new to me. What does it mean?"

❑ **56. Listen for ambiguous statements.** When you get a vague or confusing response from buyers, use "Colombo" questioning techniques. Examples:

"Can you tell me *exactly* what you mean by X?"
"Are you saying X or Y?"
"Help me understand something, please. You would do X, if we could do Y. Is that right?"

❑ **57. Listen for extreme reactions.** If a buyer responds emotionally, ask her to explain her strong reaction. "Jane, many people choose not to advertise in *XYZ* magazine, but very few get so angry about it! Can you tell me what has led you to such a strong viewpoint?"

❑ **58. Take the emotional temperature of your buyers.** Emotions play a strong role in any decision-making process. Listen for, and acknowledge, feelings. "It sounds like you're very *excited* about this expansion, but *worried* about the time frame involved. Is that right?"

❑ **59. Listen for tone of voice.** "How much?" said *inquisitively* is likely to be a legitimate request for pricing information. "How much?" said *sarcastically* can be masking many things (e.g., a preconceived idea of price, a previous bad experience). The words are the same, but the different meanings require different seller responses.

☐ **60. Listen for your buyer's risk threshold.** Low-risk tolerance language clues: "We work on consensus . . ." "Our relationships go back a long time . . ." "I don't make waves here . . ." "Who else have you done this for?" "What happens if I have problems with the system?"

Higher-risk tolerance language clues: "We do what works . . ." "Results are our number-one priority . . ." "We're living in a world of change . . ." "How fast could you implement this . . ."

☐ **61. Listen for buyers' priorities in making decisions.** Do your buyers decide on the numbers, or on the impact on other people?

Numbers language clues: "Systematic approach to our problems . . ." "Business is about numbers . . ." "What data do you have to support that?" "Step-by-step methodology . . ."

People language clues: "My team and I . . ." "I feel strongly about . . ." "Consensus is very important . . ." "I like . . ." "We look for relationships . . ."

☐ **62. Listen for client's sense of urgency.** How quickly is a client likely to act?

Act-now language clues: "The pressure is on . . ." "We just lost a big client . . ." "At this rate, we'll be off 10 percent by next year . . ." "How long will it take . . . ?"

Act-later language clues: "We check out options periodically . . ." "At some point . . ." "The committee has to meet . . ." "Send me research on . . ." "We're pretty happy . . ."

☐ **63. Listen for unreasonable expectations.** Catch problems before they start.

Buyer: "I'm really looking forward to the savings we'll realize with this system."
Seller: "What size savings are you expecting?"
Buyer. "In the neigborhood of $100,000."
Seller: (calmly) "I see. Yes, you will definitely save money in your department with the XYZ system, but the number is more likely to be in the $25 to $35,000 range. Here's why . . ."

☐ **64. Listen for questions masquerading as traps.** When you hear a question with a suspected ulterior motive or hidden agenda behind it, or where you think that no matter what answer you give you might wind up in trouble, answer with a question. Example:

Buyer: "Just how many companies our size have you dealt with?"
Seller: "Why do you ask?"

☐ **65. If you want to be heard, first listen.**

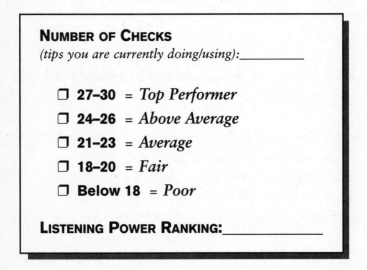

NUMBER OF CHECKS
*(tips you are currently doing/using):*_____

☐ **27–30** = *Top Performer*

☐ **24–26** = *Above Average*

☐ **21–23** = *Average*

☐ **18–20** = *Fair*

☐ **Below 18** = *Poor*

LISTENING POWER RANKING:_____

PRESENTING

"The art of being a bore is to tell everything."

—VOLTAIRE

Preparation

☐ **66. Preparation precedes success.** Who will be there? How sophisticated are they? What is the appropriate tone for this presentation? What is the client's business situation? How does your product or service solve his problems or add value to his situation? What questions and objections will your information have to address? What is the competitive situation? If the meeting is a success, what next step should he take?

☐ **67. Storyboard your presentation.** Lay out your presentation on the floor and literally walk through it. Check: Is it sequenced correctly? Does it have the right information? Are the selling points clear? Is it interesting? Does it meet your sales objective?

❐ **68. Does your presentation flow?** Transitioning words and phrases give a presentation its movement and its rhythm. Examples:

"Not only are you getting . . . but you're also saving . . ."
"In addition . . ."
"Moreover . . ."
"How do we do that? . . ."
"Here's another advantage of this system . . ."

❐ **69. Add the creative touch.** For example, you can open with a quote. If you're selling financial services, you could open your presentation with the following: "Sophie Tucker once said, 'I've been rich and I've been poor and, honey, rich is better.' " (pause)

"Today, we're going to look at three strategies to make *you* richer."
Other ways to add a dash of creativity: Share a startling fact; use props; turn your presentation into a game; ask a provocative question.

❐ **70. Visual aids or visual confusion?** Keep visuals simple, clear, easy to read, and eye-catching. Pictures, graphs, charts, and bullet points, with very few words, are most effective. The same applies to electronic media. If all people remember is the "wow" of your visual effects, but none of the message, then you may have gone overboard on the visual side of your presentation.

❐ **71. Number your pages.** If you are using any kind of notes, index cards, script, a combination of notes and pictures of your slides, number the pages. If you drop them and have to get them back into order quickly, you'll be glad you did.

❐ **72. Travel with your visuals.** Never check your slides, disks, overheads, or leave-behinds with your luggage. The one time you do you can bet they'll wind up in Portland, Maine, when your presentation is in Portland, Oregon.

❐ **73. God is in the details.** For a group presentation, what kind of meeting room will you be in? What audio/visuals will be most appropriate? Who should come from your firm? How long will you have? What's the best format for discussion? When will it be best to take questions? What material will you leave behind? Who is taking care of the logistics? Can you get into the room early to set up? Depending on the medium you're using, do you have extra cables, bulbs, pens, and extension cords? Don't leave *anything* to chance.

❐ **74. Places, please!** In team presentations, planning and rehearsing are important. Plan who will open, who will handle which sections of the presentation, who will conclude and summarize. Rehearse introductions, transitions, and questions. Identify how one team member will build on the other's comments or interrupt. Let the client see an organization that has its act together.

Mental Preparation

❐ **75. How you see yourself will affect your results.**

"To be a great champion, you must believe you are the best."

—MUHAMMAD ALI

❐ **76. Jitter Control.** Prepare for a presentation the way you would for a tennis match, football game, or swimming competition. Practice. Think positively. See yourself succeeding. Loosen up: just prior to the event, hum to warm up your voice; yawn an exaggerated yawn to open up all the throat muscles; take deep breaths and exhale very slowly to calm yourself. Smile. Walk in. Begin.

❐ **77. No one ever died of a presentation.** Do you know the story of the matador who was killed by the bull on the only day he *wasn't* nervous?

Nervousness is the rush of adrenaline. Just as that adrenaline rush helps you play better in sports, it helps you as well in a presentation. Welcome it. Let it work for you.

During the Presentation

☐ **78. Calm the butterflies.** The key is to talk to one person until you stop speaking naturally: at the end of a thought, or a sentence, or a phrase. Then, shift to another person and talk to that person, until you again come to a similar natural pause or breathing space. This gives you control of your thinking and of your breathing, which is the first thing to go when you are nervous.

☐ **79. Fear of forgetting.** If you leave something out in error, it will most likely come back to you as a question. If your mind goes blank on a point, pause, recover the thought, and say what you intended. The few seconds of your pause are hardly noticed by your group. If the thought does not come to you, admit you've lost your train of thought and move on. Invariably, it returns a little later and you can just weave the remembered point back into the presentation.

☐ **80. Don't be a slave to a script.** If you have to use a script, mark it with places where you stop and tell a story or give examples. This breaks any tendency to read and lets you engage directly with your audience in a conversational way.

❐ **81. Get early agreement on your assumptions.** In one-on-one and small group meetings, it is a good idea to begin with your understanding of the buyer's situation. Then, ask, "Is that right?" or "Has anything changed since we spoke?" or "Do you all agree?" Since your entire presentation is based on these assumptions, it is imperative that you get this feedback before you continue. If your buyer says you're wrong, STOP and go back to probing to get a revised picture of her situation. In a larger group, where it may be inappropriate to ask for an actual response, a slight pause and look at the group for silent nodding confirmation is sufficient.

❐ **82. Set the procedure for questions.** In a group presentation, tell your audience how/when you will handle questions. "Please hold your questions and I'll be glad to take them at the end" or, "As we go through this, ask your questions at any time." Tell them what to do, and most of them will take the direction.

❐ **83. Dispel objections in your presentation.** Weave the answers to objections uncovered in the probing part of your sale into your selling message.

Seller: "Sally, *earlier you said you wanted a firm experienced in your industry.* We haven't worked specifically in your industry. However, look at these projects that we did. You'll see . . ."

❒ **84. Tell and sell.** People do *not* buy features. They buy what the features of your product or services *give* them.

Weak:
"This program can be delivered in over twenty-three cities." (So what?)
Better:
"This program can be delivered in over twenty-three cities. *Since your staff is scattered across the U.S., this means you get tremendous flexibility in scheduling and savings in travel.*" (Yes!)

❒ **85. Benefit insurance.** If you want to guarantee that you're always presenting benefits, use the phrases in the examples below. They automatically shift the selling focus from your information back to benefits for the buyer.

Examples:
(Claim) "We have . . . (benefit shift) *so you get . . .*"
(Claim) "This can do . . . (benefit shift) *so you save . . .*"
(Explanation) "Our process works like this . . . (benefit shift) *which means you'll reduce* your . . . by . . . percent."

❒ **86. Story sell.** Stories are as old as the caveman. Buyers like to hear success stories. They want to know that you've seen their problems before and have solved them successfully. Buyers relate to other firms, or people, whose names they recognize and respect. Sprinkle your selling with tales of success.

❒ 87. Use Analogies. Drive your point home with a memorable analogy. For example, "Just because they are experienced, salespeople shouldn't think they are beyond precall preparation checklists. *They're like 747 airline pilots. We accept that they know how to fly, but we wouldn't want to be in a plane with them if they skipped the cockpit checklist.*"

❒ 88. Add impact to your numbers. Compare: "Our publication is read by one million people" to "Our publication is read by one million people—that's ten Super Bowls of potential buyers for your product!" Take your key numbers and translate them into easily visualized, concrete terms, meaningful to your buyer.

❒ 89. Reinforce selling points. Repeat the actual words or the spirit of your selling point when you present a block of facts or a lengthy explanation. Read the following with, and without, the last reinforcing line to hear the difference. "*365 Sales Tips* will help increase business for you. The tips are practical and they work. They cover all aspects of face-to-face selling from probing to negotiating, as well as tips on the intangibles that come from an upbeat, can-do attitude. *Bottom line: 365 Sales Tips is a good investment.*"

❑ **90. Confirm agreement with buyer.** After you make a claim or explain something and attach benefits to it, you cannot assume your buyer has accepted what you said, unless you check back with him.

Examples:
"How does this sound?"
"Are we on track here?"

❑ **91.** *"I tell you and you forget. I show you and you remember. I involve you and you understand."*

(Old Proverb)

Involve buyers in various ways in your presentation. Ask them to imagine a situation. Ask them to select an item from a list that they would like you to talk about. Have them estimate something. Have them turn to each other and discuss something. Ask a rhetorical question, which sharpens their attention, because they want to hear the answer. People understand best when they are involved.

❑ **92. Comparisons to the competition.** It is generally a bad idea to "knock" the competition. It is far smarter to bias your buyer's purchasing criteria toward *your* product or service.

Weak:
"Our product is much better than competitor A's. Their breakdown, delivery, and service records are awful."
Better:

"As you review vendors, be sure to check out breakdown, delivery, and service records, since these can cost you a fortune in downtime. Not all companies are equal in those areas. Ours has an admirable record. In fact, that's why clients renew with us regularly."

You can bet the client will check those factors out with your competitors for herself.

Personal Delivery Skills

☐ **93. Keep your energy level up.** A group responds to your conviction, passion, and enthusiasm. If these are low, they will be inattentive. If they are high, your group will be alert. The extra energy you put into presenting is like the extra energy you put into playing a sport. When you walk onto a sports field or court, your energy is at one level. As soon as the ball is in play, however, your energy and attention levels go way up. In a group presentation, you're "in play," and you need to perform at higher energy levels to keep your audience's attention.

☐ **94. Antidote for the monotone.** Movement adds inflection to your voice. Use your hands to reinforce your points as you speak. Your playing field is in front of you, at about waist level. Use your hands to list or count things on your fingers, show relationships, show movement, or for emphasis.

❑ **95. Don't be afraid of silence.** Pause after an important statement (count two beats for practice). Pause after a significant number (1-2). Pause for emphasis (1-2). Pause for drama (1-2). Pauses seem like eternities to you, but they help your buyers assimilate what you just said. Prove that to yourself by taping yourself with pauses.

❑ **96. Where go your toes, so goes your nose.** If you are presenting at an overhead screen, be aware of your toes. If they are pointed at the screen, you will wind up reading the screen and losing your audience. If your toes are pointed toward the audience, you will be able to glance at the screen to pick up your thoughts and yet still be able to turn and speak directly to the audience.

The End of the Presentation

❑ **97. Let the clients sell themselves.** After your presentation, ask clients what they think are the three best things they heard about your product or service. It's a good test of how well your message got across.

❑ **98. Summarize with the Rule of Three.** Three is a magic number. There's a rhythm to it, and we use it all the time: XYZ; ABC; red, white, and blue; Tom, Dick, and Harry; bacon, lettuce, and tomato. It's easy to remember three things. Leave people with three highlights to remember about your presentation. They will feel they understood everything you said, and they will be able to recall your selling points as easily as . . . 1-2-3.

Miscellaneous

❑ **99. Avoid "I-Strain."** The buyer, not the seller, is always the center of a sale.

Weak:
"I think X is a great product."
"I think you're just going to love it."
"I want to show you."
Better:
"*You'll* find this is a really good product."
"*Clients* love the way it works." (Buyers identify with other buyers.)
(*You,* understood) "Take a look at this."

Don't confuse personal enthusiasm with smart selling.

☐ 100. Be succinct.

Weak:

"So, we were very pleased with the results that we got last year, since it was a tough year and no one really expected to do that well. The economy was off. Our industry was off. My biggest account was down 30 percent. It was bad."

Better:

"Last year's results were an unexpected, but welcome, surprise for everyone."

More is not necessarily better. Remember, the Gettysburg Address only had 272 words.

☐ 101. Tough question? It's often difficult to respond immediately to hostile or complex questions. Give yourself time to think and to neutralize any "hot" language by paraphrasing, repeating, or acknowledging the question. Examples:

Q: "How do you explain the fiasco your firm was involved in at XYZ company?"

A: (Paraphrase) "With regard to the incident at XYZ . . ." (then answer).

Q: "Why are you recommending the 341 line over the 456 line?"

A: (Repeat) "Why the 341 line over the 456? Because . . ."

Q: "How will we pay for the extra costs of this installation?"

A. (Acknowledge) "We were particularly sensitive to the costs involved in this process. Basically, we've arranged for . . ."

☐ **102. What to do about handouts.** If you give out something at the beginning of your presentation, you lose control of people's attention. On the other hand, if you are presenting complex information, people like to make notes on the actual visual. Compromise: hand out only what you're talking about at that moment and promise a complete packet of your visuals and information at the end of the meeting.

☐ **103. Time's up!** When you are unexpectedly cut off in a presentation, jump to your summary. Even if you haven't covered everything in detail, you want to leave people with the key points of your message.

☐ **104. Gag your gags.** Avoid telling jokes. If your client doesn't find the joke funny or, worse, finds it offensive, you've created a very awkward situation. However, tasteful, spontaneous humor works. For example, a salesperson was trying to replace an existing vendor currently used by a prospective client. Early in the discussion, the salesperson said, "I know you are using vendor X. You've also heard about the good work my company does. Would you consider running a competitive test between your current vendor and myself and whoever wins will become your future supplier?" To the salesperson's amazement, the client immediately said, "Yes." Partly in shock, the salesperson just leaned back in his chair and said nothing. When the client asked "What's wrong?" the salesperson said, "Nothing. I learned a long time ago not to sell beyond the close. I just got your 'Yes,' and I'm not saying another word!" The client laughed, and the two continued to talk—about other topics. (P.S. this salesperson subsequently beat the other supplier and won all the business.)

❑ 105. Put PEP into "on the spot" presentations.

Given thirty minutes, most people can easily talk about their product or service. But can you give a crisp, provocative, compelling overview of your product in thirty seconds when you meet someone in an unexpected situation—for example, next to you on the plane on a business trip? In client meetings, can you give a provocative three-minute presentation when someone asks for it?

"PEP" is a formula for a successful mini-presentation. It basically says, Make your point, expand on it, and end on the point.

Point: "We specialize in sales-force automation to expedite a company's sales process."

Explain: "Success depends on tailoring. For example, we helped XYZ company develop a system for fifty people who are on the road almost 90 percent of the time and another for a company with two thousand reps scattered in offices around the world. Our software integrates your sales information with your research, management, and production departments."

Point: "Bottom line: we help salespeople close business faster."

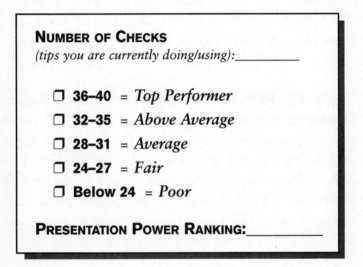

NUMBER OF CHECKS
*(tips you are currently doing/using):*_____

☐ **36–40** = *Top Performer*
☐ **32–35** = *Above Average*
☐ **28–31** = *Average*
☐ **24–27** = *Fair*
☐ **Below 24** = *Poor*

PRESENTATION POWER RANKING:_____

HANDLING OBJECTIONS

Engage mind before mouth.

General Guidelines

☐ **106. See objections as opportunities to explain and save the sale rather than as obstacles to stall the sale.**

☐ **107. No product or service is objection-proof.** There is no perfect product on the market. You don't need to eliminate all objections, only the critical ones.

☐ **108. It's your product, it's not you.** Separate the business from the personal. Buyers have a job to do. When they object, the objection is about your product or service. It is not about you.

❑ 109. Sellers don't plan to fail, but they often fail to plan. *Anticipate* objections and prepare your answers in advance. What concerns might buyers raise early in your meeting (no need? no budget?)? What product or service features will buyers likely object to as you get deeper into discussion?

❑ 110. Behind every objection is someone who is either misinformed, confused, skeptical, angry (your last delivery was late!), **or right** (your product does *not* come in the color the buyer wants).

If misinformed, educate.
If skeptical, prove otherwise.
If angry, show what has been done to change the problem.
If right, acknowledge and outweigh with other benefits.

Getting Past No

❑ 111. Don't get stuck on early objections. On first calls, it is fairly common to encounter an objection shortly after you and your buyer exchange amenities. Since there has been little discussion at that point, it is difficult for the seller to counter with any compelling response. While the seller may choose to address the concern head-on, one alternative is to respond briefly and then refocus the conversation back onto the buyer.

Buyer: "I hear your investment performance has slipped quite a bit."

(Brief response)

Seller: "Yes, this has been a tough year. However, our longer-term performance has been quite good and our clients appreciate that continuous growth."

(Refocus the conversation)

"Before we get into performance details, tell me a bit about your investment goals."

☐ **112. Ask to put an early objection "on hold."** It is not unreasonable to request a delay in discussing the buyer's early concern. Just give your buyer a reason that is in **her** interest to accept the delay.

Buyer: "I understand that you're a New York–based firm. That's a problem because we are located in five cities."

Seller: "*Can we talk about that in a few minutes? First, let's look at what's most important to you, which is your overall objectives for next year,* and then we can come back to how we are able to service your company. My understanding is . . . Tell me more about that."

☐ **113. Humor your way out of an early objection.** A good laugh between two people can often redirect your buyer's objection to a positive discussion.

Buyer: "I'm not interested. We're not planning our budgets yet."

Seller: "Just my luck! You know, I always arrive on the day *before* or *after* budget planning. I've never arrived on the *exact* day of planning!"

(Buyer chuckles.)

Seller: "But, let's say I had arrived on your planning day, what issues will be most important to you for this project?"

Managing Objections

☐ **114. Don't Argue. Ask.** Don't make buyers feel they are wrong for their opinions. The more you argue, the more they'll fight to justify their position. Instead, ask questions to uncover the thinking behind the objection. For example, "What leads you to that conclusion?" or "That's an interesting observation. Why do you say that?"

☐ **115. Probe for the real concern.** You cannot address what you don't understand.

Buyer: "You're not really right."

Seller: *"Can you tell me exactly what you mean?"*

Buyer: "Your people have no experience in my industry."

Seller: *"Which means . . . ?"*

Buyer: "You'll never be able to do the job."

Seller: *"So, your concern is our competence?"*

Buyer: "No, the issue is your ability to meet our April deadline."

Seller: *"I see. It's the deadline, not our expertise. Is that right?"*
Buyer: "Yes."

This process requires p-a-t-i-e-n-c-e, strong probing, and strong listening skills.

❐ **116. Isolate the uncovered objection.** Isolate the stated objection to see if there is more to it.

Seller: "So your real concern is meeting your deadline. Is that right?"
Buyer: "Yes."
(Isolate)
Seller: *"Is there anything else besides* our ability to make your April target that concerns you?"

(If no, you've got the real obstacle to your sale. If yes, then you've allowed additional objections to surface, with which you'll deal.)

❐ **117. Be agreeable, without agreeing.** When a buyer has dug in his heels on an objection, or is very emotional about his concern, use an acknowledging phrase—a mental bridge—to lead him from his hardened position to the possibilities in your response.

Buyer: "Yes, that's correct. There's no way I can leave myself open to missed deadlines!"

(Bridge)

Seller: "*Let me clarify that*. Here's how we will do that."
Or, "*Clearly, meeting your deadline is very important.*
Here's what we will do." (And, then, the seller gives the
answer.)

☐ **118. Avoid the killer phrase "I think."** It leads to a
win-lose situation. Instead, use an acknowledging phrase
before your answer.

Buyer: "I don't think you have the manpower for this
project."

Weak:

Seller: "Oh, **I think** we do."

Buyer: Well, I don't.

Seller: "But I can . . ."

Better:

Seller: (Acknowledging) "Manpower is really important."
(Answer) "Here's what you'll find with us . . ."

☐ **119. Switch: Turn a negative objection into a
positive selling point.** Use the objection itself as the rationale for overcoming the objection. This completely surprises your buyer and it casts a totally new, positive light
on what he thought was a negative.

Buyer: "You're too rich for my budget."

(Switch)

Seller: *"That's exactly why you should invest in this system.* If you have limited funds, you want the system that will last the longest and give you your greatest return, and the XYZ system does that!"

☐ **120. Check back for acceptance of your response to the buyer's objection.** After addressing objections, confirm that your buyer has changed her views.

Buyer: "My concern is that you have no experience in our industry."

Seller: "Is there anything else besides the experience that concerns you?"

Buyer: "No, that's it."

Seller: "Let me put your mind to rest about that. We . . ." (Checking)

Seller: *"Does that make sense now?"*

Other examples of check-back questions are: Is that clearer now? Did you realize that? Do you agree? Are we back on track? How does that sound? What do you think?

Special Situations

☐ **121. Satisfy the data-demon.** For buyers who are information-driven, logical, organized, step-by-step thinkers, respond in a way that respects their style. (Very often, their tempo is slower than yours.)

Buyer: "The dental plan is missing . . ."

Seller (speaking in a measured pace): "Let's *examine* that. *On the one hand,* the dental plan is missing . . . *On the other hand,* you are getting the best . . . , . . . , . . . , and . . . *On balance,* it would seem to make sense to go with it. Do you agree?"

☐ **122. Satisfy the strong relationship-oriented buyer.** For a buyer who operates from his feelings, empathize and share a story.

Buyer: "The dental plan is missing . . ."

Seller: "*I understand how you feel. That's what XYZ company felt at first, but when they took a closer look at the total package, they found that overall it was really good for their people, and they are very happy with it.* Let me show you what I mean . . . How do you *feel* about the plan now?"

☐ **123. Defuse the angry objector.** Clients with bad experiences need to verbalize their anger over a past disappointment or perceived mistreatment. They need to have their feelings validated first, before they will listen to any further selling.

(Be sympathetic.)

Seller: "I'm sorry that happened. This clearly caused you a great deal of trouble and inconvenience."

Buyer: "You're darn right it did!"

Seller: "It shouldn't have happened."
(Show how you/your company is fixing the situation.)
"This is what we're doing to correct the situation. Is that satisfactory?" Or, "What would you like us to do to remedy the situation?"

Follow up frequently to see that things are okay. Expect that it will take some time to rebuild trust with this buyer.

The Price Objection

☐ **124. "You're too expensive."** When buyers say your product or service is too expensive, ask, "Relative to what?" Sometimes, your buyer is comparing your product or service to an inferior competitor's offering. Sometimes, the buyer is thinking of a price he received in another part of the country, under different circumstances, in different quantities, etc. Before you can respond to the buyer, you need to understand the source of his price objection.

☐ **125. Is it really price?** Qualify the price objection for the same reason that you would isolate any objection to make sure it is the real objection and not a smoke screen.

Buyer: "You're too expensive."
Seller: (Isolate) "If money were not an issue, would we be doing business?"

If the answer is yes, find other sources of funds for them; e.g., from another budget or from the competitor's share, or offer to bill in a different time period. If the answer is no, then the real objection is probably something else.

❐ **126. Price confidence is critical.** Many buyers have to justify your price to their superiors. If you don't communicate complete conviction in the value of what you're selling, they will feel uncomfortable selling you and your products or services up the line.

Weak:
Seller: "Uh, well, it is on the, uh, high side, but, uh, it's, uh, really worth it."
Better:
Seller: "Clients use our service because it is 100 percent reliable. And that's what you want. Isn't it?"

❐ **127. Sell value, not cost.** Clearly demonstrate how what you are selling adds to or multiplies some factor for your buyers; e.g., triples their productivity.

Break down large cost figures into bite-size comparisons. For example, to an automobile advertiser whose cars sell on average for $40,000 each, a $300,000 advertising campaign is only seven and a half cars. For a small-business owner whose average sale is $4,000, a $4,000 direct-mail campaign to a thousand prospects is only $1 a person, or the cost of one new piece of business, which he is more than likely to get from the mailing. Translating large numbers into concrete, meaningful terms makes the buyer's investment easier to accept.

□ 128. Counter the price objection with a comparison. Comparisons help buyers to see the value point you are making.

Buyer: "You're too expensive."

Seller: "Joe, if you were going to take a plane trip, would you want the cheapest pilot or the best pilot flying your plane?"

Buyer: "Obviously, the best!"

Seller: "Exactly. The same is true with our product. Our customers want the best. They like knowing they'll always have inventory on hand. Isn't that what you want?"

□ 129. Counter price with fear of loss. Show what your buyer will be losing by not using your product. Simply ask,

What's the price of missing the market?

What's the price of using unreliable equipment?

Do you really want to put your equipment and people at risk?

Do you really want to cede the market to your competition?

The "No Need" Objection

❑ **130. Ask a question.** Don't become adversarial. A question will help open up new possibilities in your buyer's mind.

Buyer: "We're happy with our present system."
Weak:
Seller: "But, we can really bring improvements to what you're doing."
Buyer: "But, I think you're offering a similar solution."
Seller: "But, you don't realize . . ."
Buyer: "But . . ."
Seller: "But . . ."
Better:
Seller: "What do you like about your current system?"
Buyer: "I like its speed, high quality, and low cost."
Seller: "What would it mean to you if you could increase the speed?"
Buyer: "A lot. How could you do that?"
Seller: "In our system, we . . ."

The Negative, Nonresponsive Buyer

❑ **131. Be honest.** Selling is a relationship between two people. Share your feelings.

Seller: "Mr. Buyer, I really believe my product can provide tremendous value to you, and I have done everything I

know to show that. But I've obviously failed. Help me.
Where have I failed?"
(Often, the buyer will say:) "It isn't that you've failed. It's
just that . . ."

You now have the real objection.

☐ **132. Make a startling statement.** One nontradi-
tional way to get a nonresponsive, negative buyer talking
is to say, very pleasantly, "Mr. Buyer, perhaps, you're not
ready for my product." This generally surprises the buyer
who is likely to ask, indignantly, "What do you mean?!"
Explain, in a very understanding tone of voice, that your
clients seek first-rate results and recognize that quality has
a price. However, if all this buyer can manage now is the
lower-quality alternative, that's fine. Often, the buyer's response is, "Quality is not the issue. The fact is . . ."

Da-Dum! The real objection emerges.

☐ **133. Question the meeting.** Politely ask, "If you are
so set against my product, why did you agree to see me
today?" Very often, their response is, "I'm not set against
it. I just have trouble with your . . ."

Voilà! The real objection surfaces.

❐ **134. Reverse roles.** When all you are hearing is "no," invite the buyer into your problem.

Seller: "Mr. Buyer, if we were to change places, what would you say to me to persuade you of the value of my product for your company?"

Buyer: "Well, if you could do something about your . . ."

There it is! You found the real objection.

The "I'll Think About It" Objection

❐ **135. Know who has the problem.** At the end of a call, if a client is not committing, avoid asking, "What's your problem with XYZ product?" The client doesn't have a problem. *You* have a problem. You haven't sold effectively enough. Instead, ask, "What issues about product XYZ would you like me to explain further?" Once you can respond successfully to those, you and your buyer will be ready to move on to the next step in the business sales cycle.

❐ **136. Ask the "scale" question.** When a client says he has to think about it, one option is to ask, "I appreciate that you want to review this material. Let me ask you, if, based on our discussion so far, you had to decide right *now,* on a scale of 1 to 5, with 1 being 'no way' and 5 being 'absolutely,' where are you in your thinking?" An answer of anything less than a 5 and you ask, "What will it take to make that number a 5?"

❑ 137. Bring the objection up yourself. When you suspect the buyer is uncomfortable admitting the truth, bring up the suspected objection yourself. Say, "I see you're not sure. Is it the . . . ?" and you name what you think is the unspoken obstacle to doing business. Very often that will cause the buyer's real concern to surface.

❑ 138. Summarize to overcome a stall. Tie up the loose ends of your discussion with your buyer to make any lingering objections come to the surface.

1. Summarize the agreed-upon benefits of your product
2. Get agreement to these, and then
3. Ask, "What did I leave out?"

That often gets the unspoken concern to pop out of the buyer.

❑ 139. Offer to work with your buyer. When he says "I'll think it over," suggest, "Let's think out loud together. What specific points do you want to review?" This gives you a chance to deal with the remaining objections.

❒ **140. The "rehearsal" response.** A variation of "I'll think it over" is "I have to talk it over with other people." Ask, "What questions do you think they will have?" Then, as you hear those questions, ask your client, "What will you say?" Help him with the answers.

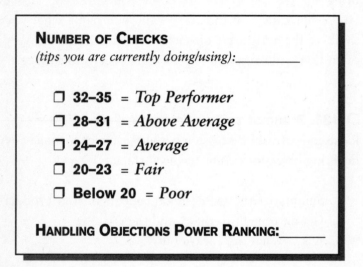

NUMBER OF CHECKS
*(tips you are currently doing/using):*_____

❒ **32–35** = *Top Performer*
❒ **28–31** = *Above Average*
❒ **24–27** = *Average*
❒ **20–23** = *Fair*
❒ **Below 20** = *Poor*

HANDLING OBJECTIONS POWER RANKING:_____

CLOSING AND FOLLOW-THROUGH

The close at the end of a call is like the kiss at the end of a good date: the natural outcome of a positive interaction.

Definition of "Closing"

☐ **141. A closing is any action step that advances the sales process to the next stage.** That step can be a request for an actual order, a second meeting with that buyer to present additional information, a meeting with other decision-makers, permission to do a needs analysis, agreement to attend a demonstration or a plant tour, permission to use your buyer's endorsement of your product or service with other people in the company. In all cases, *the buyer is agreeing to do something* as a result of your call.

A Closing Attitude

☐ **142. Expect to do business.** Go to a party expecting a good time, and you generally enjoy yourself. Go with a negative attitude, and you generally don't. If you walk into a call worried, uncertain, and unprepared, the call is destined to fail. Be prepared, looking forward to the meeting and expecting to do business, and you're likely to meet with success.

Timing

☐ **143. Don't force the closing.** People will buy when they feel good about dealing with you; when they believe in the ability of your product to solve their problem; when they feel that the price is fair for what they are getting; and when they have confidence in your company to deliver service and quality. Be sure you've covered all these bases before you attempt to get a commitment.

☐ **144. Respect a buyer's need to review.** Sometimes, when buyers say they have to "think it over," they are not stalling. They really do need time to review your material. The best "closing step" is to determine a comfortable time frame to follow up and schedule that meeting. For example, you might say, "Fine. Can we set up a meeting, say, for next Tuesday to discuss any final questions you might have?"

❒ **145. Raise your own objection.** When you want to see if, on balance, your buyer is on your side and is ready to move forward, raise a small objection yourself.

Buyer: "Yes, yes, this sounds good."
Seller: "Good. Of course, we'll have to wait to schedule the needs analysis until my research team returns in two weeks from overseas. Will that throw cold water on our doing business?"
Buyer: "No."
Seller: "Are you sure?"
Buyer: "Absolutely. I'll wait. I like what I've seen."

❒ **146. Recognize "buy" signals.** When people are ready to be kissed, they do things to signal that readiness: they pucker up, get quiet, lean forward, etc. When buyers are ready to move forward and commit, they, too, signal their readiness. They ask specific questions about timing, delivery, and implementation. They become quiet. They look seriously at your literature. They say they like what they're hearing.

How to Close

❒ **147. The simplest closing.** When the sales call has gone well and it's clear that the buyer is very interested in your product or service, say, "Great. What's our next step?"

☐ **148. Keep the closing short.** When your buyer has clearly indicated her satisfaction with your proposal, respond *briefly*.

Buyer: "This sounds good."
Weak:
Seller: "Terrific. Should I send the proposal to you or John? You're really going to like this . . . Everyone does . . . It's . . . Furthermore, blah, blah, blah . . ."
Better:
Seller: "Terrific. Should I send the proposal to you or to John?"
(Wait for buyer to respond).
Buyer: "Send it to John and copy me."
Seller: "Fine, you'll both have it by Tuesday."

☐ **149. "Loose lips sink ships"—and sales.** After signing a deal, it can be dangerous to continue selling.

Seller: "Fine. We'll take good care of you. You'll really like John, our new Production head. He's a great guy."
Buyer: "New Production head? Wait a minute. I'm not sure I want to be a guinea pig on someone's learning curve!"
Seller: "Oh, he's very experienced. He's—"
Buyer: "I don't think so. I'll have to review this."

Bye-bye, deal.

☐ **150. Make it easy for the buyer to say "Yes!"** It can be confusing and intimidating for a buyer to agree to a package of next steps. However, it is usually easy to agree to one specific next step.

Weak:
"The next steps are A, B, C, D, and E. Shall we go ahead?"
Better:
"The next steps are A, B, C, D, and E. The *immediate* next step, however, is A. *Shall we go ahead with that?*"

☐ **151. Close with a straightforward request for the business.** When the conversation between you and the buyer has been positive and the buyer is enthusiastic, one way to close is simply to ask for the business.

Buyer: "This sounds really good."
Weak:
Seller: "Yes, it is a great service. Our clients really like it. Here's something else you'll like about it . . ."
Better:
Seller: "Yes, it is. Our clients really like it. *Do you want me to write up a contract?*"

☐ **152. Close by assuming the next step.** Once the buyer has indicated his wish to commit, another way to close is to assume the business and simply clarify the next step for implementation.

Buyer: "This will do it."
Weak:
Seller: "You're right. Based on what we discussed, this is your best choice."
Better:
Seller: "Yes, this is your best choice. *When do you want to start the needs analysis?*"

◻ **153. Close on a checking question.** You've uncovered an objection, isolated it, given your response. Now, close.

"So, *if* this makes sense, *can we set up a meeting with the committee?*"
"So, *if* you agree, then we can ship as early as Monday. *Is that a good day for you?*"

◻ **154. Close on an objection.** Turn a potential block to your sale into a reason to buy your service or product.

Buyer: "Your three-month waiting period for delivery is about thirty days too long."
Weak:
Seller: "It will be difficult to change that, but I can try."
Better:
Seller: "*If I can get the delivery for you in two months, will you commit to the business today?*"

❐ **155. Close on a buyer's question.** A buyer's question is often a signal that he is ready to do business with you, if a particular condition can be met. Recognize this interest to move forward.

Buyer: "Is page one available?"
Weak:
Seller: "Yes, it is."
Better:
Seller: *"If it is, do you want it?"* or, *"No, it isn't, but if you can have your ad placed on the back cover, would you like that position?"*

Special Situations

❐ **156. Help wavering clients decide with "on balance" thinking.** When clients can't make up their minds, think through the decision-making process with them.

Seller: "Mr. Client, on the one hand, you've had good service from your current supplier and you like the people personally. On the other hand, considering what you said about how your business is changing, you like our . . . , . . . , . . . and . . . Right?"
Client: "Absolutely."
Seller: "Then, *on balance,* doesn't it make sense to switch?"
Buyer: "Yes, it does."
Seller: "To get started, I'll send you a written proposal to sign. Okay?"
Buyer: "Yes, that will be fine."

❐ **157. Close with testimonials.** When prospects are close to buying, but not convinced, be prepared to present a list of references or testimonial letters to reassure them. Stronger still, have an existing client call the prospect on your behalf. This little extra proof of your firm's ability to perform is often all it takes to get a client to move from *maybe* to *okay*.

❐ **158. Give procrastinating clients a reason to commit now.**

Examples:

1. "Rates are going up next year. Sign up today to save the 6 percent increase."
2. "Inventory is limited. To guarantee that you can get . . . , we need to know by Monday."
3. "Only three spaces are left. If you want to participate, you'd be wise to commit today."
4. "We ship tomorrow, so your decision today is critical."

❐ **159. Close with the calendar.** When your proposal includes a series of steps over a long time period, it is easy for the buyer to lose a sense of urgency to act. Create that urgency by squeezing the future back to the present. Seller: "Ruth, you said earlier that you want a June installation, which is six months from now. Since it takes one month for you to . . . , two months for us to . . . , and two weeks to . . . , *we would need to get started by February first. Do you agree?"*

☐ **160. Avoid the spinning-wheel syndrome.** Clients who are very relationship oriented are often positive about everything you say, and they will meet with you and take your calls, but they don't sign. Appeal to their emotions. "Help me, Mr. Buyer. I'm in trouble with my boss because we haven't signed this contract yet. Help me." This often brings out the real obstacle to the sale and allows you to take the steps necessary to close the business.

☐ **161. The "waiter" strategy.** Endless requests for information delay closing business. Do what waiters do. They eliminate extra trips to the bar by anticipating all possible drink requests by a customer.

Customer: "Scotch, please."
Waiter: "House brand okay? On the rocks? Straight up? With a twist?"
In selling,
Client: "Can you get me A?"
Seller: *"Will you also want B, C and D?"*
Client: "Yes."
Seller: "Fine. *What else will you need to make a decision?"*

Smooth Follow-Through

☐ **162. Avoid buyer's remorse.** After they commit to a course of action, whether it's buying a house, getting married, changing jobs, or buying your services, most people have some doubts. A little reassurance helps.

Seller: "When do you want to start?"
Buyer: "Next week."
Seller: "Fine. We'll take good care of this for you."

☐ **163. Do a "how we work together" plan with clients.** After you and the buyer have agreed to work together, establish in writing *who* does *what* and *when* in your organization *and* in theirs. Include specific names, due dates, and checkpoints. Closing won you the business. A smooth follow-through will keep it for you.

☐ **164. Beware of overexcited buyers.** Buyers who are long on enthusiasm are often short on follow-up. With this kind of buyer, protect yourself. Get the name and phone number of the person who will actually implement the details of your agreement.

☐ **165. Determine client contact comfort zones.** As part of your follow-through, ask clients their preferences for timing and frequency of contact. Not every client wants to hear from you weekly, and not every client is comfortable waiting to hear from you every third month. If you assume a certain contact pattern and you're wrong, the former client will feel annoyed and the latter client will feel ignored.

☐ **166. Make friends with your client's secretary.** Administrative details inevitably crop up after a contract is signed. You need a troubleshooting ally at the client's place of business. Give the client's secretary your card with the name of your secretary on it. Have your secretary call and introduce him/herself. Do everything possible to ensure easy communication between your office and your client's office.

☐ **167. Keep the business growing.** Visit clients regularly. Develop multiple contacts on all levels. Be aware of their needs. Get referrals to other divisions. Be a source of new solutions to their problems as they arise.

Closing the Multi-Buyer Sale

☐ **168. A committee buy is a committee sell.** See everyone who can affect the decision to buy your product.

1. *Stakeholder:* the one whose bottom line is at risk
2. *Finance* person: the one who controls the budget
3. *User(s):* the person/people who will use your product

4. *Screen:* the one who is recommending your product or service

☐ **169. Rehearse your "screen."** This is the person who checks that your product or service meets the specs, or requirements, for a job. She is not usually the decision maker. When your screen says she'll recommend your product, ask (1) what the decision maker will like about your product, (2) what he will dislike, (3) what this person will say to the decision maker to counter the dislikes. You, of course, help her craft the most persuasive answers.

☐ **170. Make sure your "screen" has the right script.** When you can't get to the decision maker and your buyer will be recommending you, be sure to send a letter to your contact restating the specific benefits of your product in the most persuasive terms possible. (If appropriate, copy the decision maker as well.)

Lost Business

☐ **171. When "No" is "No."** Find out why you lost the business by asking for advice. People generally don't like to criticize, but they love to give advice.

Weak:
"Joan, why did we lose the business?"
Better:

"Joan, I'm sorry we won't be working together, and I hope you'll invite us in next go-around. Just as you are always striving to improve your services to your clients, so are we. *What advice would you give me for the next time to make our services more attractive to you?*"

❒ **172. Stay in touch.** A company's needs change. People change jobs. Priorities shift. Check in after your competitor has delivered his product or service. Ask how things went. Share some new information about your company. Periodically, send notes telling about your company's success. Staying in touch positions you favorably for unexpected opportunities.

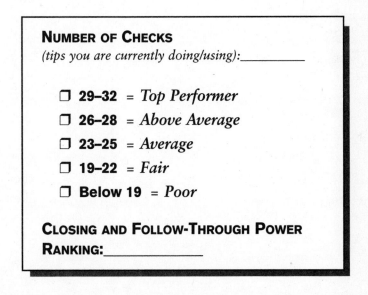

NUMBER OF CHECKS
*(tips you are currently doing/using):*_____

❒ **29–32** = *Top Performer*
❒ **26–28** = *Above Average*
❒ **23–25** = *Average*
❒ **19–22** = *Fair*
❒ **Below 19** = *Poor*

CLOSING AND FOLLOW-THROUGH POWER RANKING:_____

NEGOTIATING

"You cannot shake hands with a clenched fist."

—INDIRA GANDHI

☐ **173. Make the sale first. Then, negotiate.** A buyer must be sold on your product or service first, before you engage in negotiations. If your buyer thinks your product is fundamentally inferior to the competition, then you have a selling problem with that buyer, not a negotiating problem.

☐ **174. Negotiating is a fact of life.** Negotiating is more and more a legitimate way of doing business in many industries. You will have better results when you:

1. see the negotiating process as an opportunity to solve a puzzle with your client rather than to fight a war against him/her, and
2. prepare properly for it.

❐ **175. Do not look for absolute answers.** All negotiations are situational. For example, if winning an account means you will open up a whole new line of business, you might negotiate very differently than if you are dealing with a small account in your strongest area, where you are the leader in the field. So, in answer to What do you do when . . . ? The response must be: It depends on the situation.

❐ **176. Win-win is the way to go.** Since you will be dealing with clients on a repeat basis, always aim for a win-win result. Recognize that you will have differences on the issues, but that you want to keep your relationship with these people positive.

❐ **177. Knowledge is power.** The more you know, the stronger you will be in a negotiation.

Planning

❐ **178. Write down what you know.** List:

1. Your interests (what you want)
2. Your buyer's interests (what you think he wants)
3. All the background facts of his business situation
4. Different options you can offer, depending on volume, delivery terms, etc.

5. Small things you can trade to make the deal work (e.g., flexibility of delivery dates, any ancillary services)
6. Your bottom line

☐ **179. Value is in the eye of the beholder.** No matter how silly they may seem, list *all* the things important to you and those that could be important to your buyer. Anything that has value to someone is negotiable: time extensions, underwriting costs, early shipments, testimonials, share of market, exclusivity, introductions to key people, free training, hot-line support, reports, access to databases, speakers at meetings, tickets, etc. These can make the difference between a deal and no deal.

☐ **180. Have a backup date for the prom.** In high school, you would have been less anxious about asking out one person to the prom if you knew you had someone else who would also accept your invitation. In negotiating, have a backup plan; e.g., you'll bring in the boss, go to another account, go above your buyer, walk. With a backup, you'll feel less anxious and be more persistent, because you will be less desperate for the business.

☐ **181. Think carefully about the other person.** People are the most important variable in a negotiation. Everyone has different motivations, personal needs, and ways of interacting. If you had to negotiate with your boss, your spouse, and a friend, you would most likely have a different strategy for each one. Always work to get the best results for your company, but never forget that people are a critical factor in negotiating and plan accordingly.

☐ **182. Think through your strategy.** Using the information you write down about a negotiation, determine your strategy.

1. What tone will you set for the meeting (friendly, businesslike, other)?
2. What will you offer and in what order (your best options first, or moderately good options first and "sweeteners" later)?
3. How will you handle any pressure (threats, ultimatums, silence)?
4. How do you want your buyer to feel at the end of the meeting?

Mental Readiness

☐ **183. Believe.** Do you (A) really believe your product adds value to your clients, *or* (B) do you think the competition is just as good? Do you (A) speak with confidence and conviction, *or* (B) are you tentative as you justify prices and terms? Are you (A) willing to walk away from a bad deal, *or* (B) are you desperate for the business? If you answered all (A)s, you're ready. If you answered even one (B), stay home.

☐ **184. The ultimate power.** To be willing to walk away from unacceptable terms is the ultimate psychological power in a negotiation.

☐ **185. Aim high.** If you ask for 50 percent of a client's budget, you will get no more than 50 percent. If you ask for 100 percent of his budget, you might get 70, 80, or 100 percent.

Opening a Negotiation

☐ **186. Establish equality with your buyer.** "Mr. Buyer, I'm looking forward to working with you. Let's look at the issues here and work out an agreement that makes sense for *both* of us."

☐ **187. Bring your buyer into the process immediately.** "Let's review the issues: what you want, what we want, and *how we can work this out together. Okay?*"

☐ **188. Separate interests from demands.** A demand is: "I want reports weekly." The interest behind this demand could be: "I'm afraid I'll lose control on my investment." Ask buyers: "What is behind your demand/ request?" or "Why is that important to you?" Specific demands often cannot be satisfied, but buyers' interests can usually be satisfied in other ways.

❑ **189. All interests are not equal.** Ask buyers for their priorities. Ask *why* these are important. Their answers will give you the flexibility you need to work toward an agreement.

❑ **190. Avoid a one-issue negotiation.** A one-issue exchange is haggling. The likelihood of a successful agreement is increased when there are many items on the table that can be modified and traded.

Buyer: "It's issue X alone!"
Seller: "Let's assume we agree on issue X. *What else is important to you?*" or,
"Let me write that down. *Now, what else is important to you?*"

❑ **191. Give a clear message about early price demands.** "If you expect my firm to be the low price bidder, then we might as well shake hands and part company friends right now. However, if you want value for your money, then let's continue talking and see what else we can do, because, as you know, our clients have improved their productivity by as much as 50 percent with our products."

❑ **192. Ride the range <u>you</u> arrange.** When a buyer sets a range—e.g., he wants a 25 to 30 percent discount— if you accept that range, you'll wind up settling between 25 and 30 percent. Instead, set your own range. "For the right amount of business, we do offer discounts, but they are usually in the 15 to 20 percent range, depending on volume." Now, the range for discussion is 15 to 30 percent and you have a chance of holding to a discount lower than 25 percent.

Navigating Through a Negotiation

❐ **193. Be clear.** Avoid mixed messages in what you are saying and what you mean.

Buyer: "Is that the best you can do?"
Weak:
Seller: "I think so. This is very good value that you're getting. And we don't usually do better than the price you have. I mean, I'd like to help, but, uh, that would be difficult."
Better:
Seller: "Yes."

❐ **194. Move s-l-o-w-l-y.** Good negotiators take their time. Think. Pause. Take time to calculate. Make a phone call. Ask a question about something said earlier. If necessary, suggest a break to check things out and return another day. Rushing leads to bad decisions.

❐ **195. Create value.** Things are only as important as you make them: When you offer something, make it special by pointing out (1) the uniqueness of specific features, (2) how much time and effort it would cost the buyer to do this himself, (3) how hard it was for you to get . . . for him, or (4) what the comparable value is in dollars. Things easily won have little value in the buyer's mind and just encourage him to keep asking for more.

☐ **196. Promote collaboration.** Bring your potential adversary to the same problem-solving side of the table with you:

1. *That's an interesting idea. Let's build on that.* Suppose we did . . . and you did . . .
2. *I understand your need to get the best price.* What if you did . . . and we did . . . ?
3. *Good point. Take it one step further.* We'll . . . if you can . . .

☐ **197. Persist, with justification.** If you can justify your terms, it is not necessary to change them.

Seller: "That will be $55,000."
Buyer: "You must be joking. I'll only pay $40,000."
Weak:
Seller: "How about $48,000?"
Better:
Seller: "$55,000 is a very fair price. Your specs are very unusual and it will take us 20 percent more time to build.

Now, if you want to amend the first-phase specs, you can save $5,000. Otherwise, $55,000 is the best price."

❑ **198. Babble is bad.** Make your offer and be quiet.

Weak:
"If you can commit to $100,000, then I can get that position in the paper for you. It's a really great position. Everyone sees it. I love it. It's really good. Really."
Better:
"If you can commit to $100,000, then I can get that position in the paper for you. It's an excellent position."

❑ **199. Trade.** If you're going to give something, *get* something.

Seller: "Ms. Buyer, if you can give us flexibility on delivery, I can guarantee you the customized color you want." Or "Ms. Buyer, what can you do for us, if we can get you that customized color?"

❑ **200. Raise the stakes.** Suppose you are negotiating 500 cases of goods. The discussion is nearing the end, and your buyer is pushing you for an additional 10 percent discount. Turn the tables and say, "10 percent? Make it 750 cases and you have a deal!"

You have nothing to lose and everything to gain.

Handling Pressure Tactics

❐ **201. Recognize pressure tactics.** All are designed to intimidate you and get a better deal for the buyer. These include:

* Ultimatums
* Guidelines ("Our policy is not to pay rate increases.")
* Silence
* Price
* Commodity ("You're all the same.")
* Time ("I need it today.")
* Flinching (feigned shock or outrage at your offer)
* Nibble (after agreement, "And, of course, training is included, right?")

Deal with them and redirect the dialogue to a solution.

❐ **202. Four ways to turn coal to diamonds.** Pressure tactics don't have to kill your negotiation or cause you to give away the store.

1. You can explain the value of your offer and hold your ground.
2. You can trade.
3. You can deflect with sarcasm or humor.
4. You can create your own pressure by playing up an advantage of yours (limited supply, e.g.).

All four let your buyers know that you see through their tactics and that you intend to see this negotiation through with them.

❐ **203. Handle ultimatums.** Depending on the circumstances, when buyers say "Give me X or the deal is off," there are at least four possible responses:

1. Summarize and refocus to get to a solution. "Ultimatums don't get us what we want. Let's step back for a minute and see where we are."
2. Trade. "I'll do . . . if you can increase your commitment by . . . Do we have a deal?"
3. Silence. The buyer will often back off and say, "Well, the deal isn't off, but I do need a sweetener here."
4. Agree that you're deadlocked, suggest that you both think about other ways of reaching agreement, and schedule another meeting to share those ideas.

❐ **204. Handle the "guideline" tactic.** In response to your buyer's citing her company's purchasing guidelines:

1. Be straightforward. "And our guidelines say we charge for setup."
2. Deflect: "I'm sure the guidelines don't say to jeopardize this project. Let's see what else we can do to make this work. Suppose you . . . and we . . . How's that?"

❐ **205. Handle the "silence" tactic.** This is one of the most popular hard-bargaining negotiating tactics. Assess the person and the situation and respond in any of these ways:

1. Return the silence. Let the other person talk first.
2. Treat it lightly: "Very good! Which negotiating course did you attend?!"
3. Say quietly, "What are you thinking?"

In all cases, you are signaling that you know what is happening and that the tactic is not working.

❐ **206. Handle the "price" tactic.** When a buyer claims better prices or higher discounts from your competition, depending on your assessment of the situation, you can:

1. Use logic. "You get what you pay for. This is what you're getting with us." Then, review the benefits of your offer and be quiet.
2. Use humor. If you think you are being toyed with, treat the tactic lightly: *"Only 20 percent?"*
3. Be empathetic. Then, trade: "I understand you need to get the most from your budget. You can get a better discount if you increase your order to . . . (or, pay in full in advance, or, guarantee your order for another year)."
4. Reassure. "Mr. Buyer, you are getting the same price as everyone else. If you like, you can call other customers who are buying exactly the same thing."

☐ **207. Handle the "commodity" tactic.** When the buyer claims, "You're all the same!" you can:

1. Clarify. "Why do you say that?"
2. Flinch. "Come on! You know that's not true!"
3. Use an analogy. "Jack, just as there are differences between your tool company and your competitors, so too there are unique differences between XXX Communications Company and the others in the industry. That's why so many firms use us. So, no, we are not all the same."

☐ **208. Handle the "time" tactic.** This is designed to give you less thinking time and to get better results for the buyer. Rather than panic:

1. Test the deadline. "I was just leaving and won't be back until six P.M. Can I get it to you tomorrow?" (They usually say yes.)
2. Test their time line. "If I get it to you today, are you deciding today?" (No.) "Good, because I can't get it to you; my boss is out of town until Tuesday."
3. If you think the time demand is real, say, "Then, let me ask you these key questions . . ." and ask your questions.

☐ **209. Handle the "flinch" tactic.** Shocked or indignant, the buyer says, "I don't think you understand. We're Big Shot Company XYZ!" You can:

1. Flinch back and redirect the dialogue: "And we're XYZ Company! Let's see how else we can make this work. Suppose you did . . . and we did . . ."
2. Reverse the flinch: "And that's *exactly* why you want to use us, because you're the best and we can do . . . , . . . , and . . . for you. And isn't that what you want?!"

☐ **210. Handle the "nibble" tactic.** The deal is done and, as you're leaving, the buyer asks for something extra; e.g., free training. You can:

1. Be a little theatrical: "Mr. Buyer, we just spent an hour working this out. You don't want to open this up again for the training, do you???"
2. Be straightforward: "Sorry, Sam, if you want training, that will cost . . ."
3. Trade up: "If you guarantee the contract for an extra year, I'll see if I can get approval to give you the training for free."

Do not just give in!

☐ **211. How to avoid panicking.** When you feel yourself becoming anxious, or the discussion is getting away from you, or things are moving too quickly, or you need time to think, *stop and summarize*. Summarize as often as necessary. It keeps both you and your buyer on track and gives the negotiation process necessary breathing room.

Ending a Negotiation

❐ **212. Watch for agreement signals.** Watch for buyers suddenly picking up a pen and making calculations, asking implementation questions, doubling back to a question on an offer you made earlier, producing new solutions to a deadlock, or for a change in tempo—either increased silence as he is thinking or a barrage of questions as he is moving toward a decision.

❐ **213. Close definitively.** There are three simple ways to close a negotiation:

1. Make your offer and be quiet: "Okay, for a year's supply of . . . , the price is . . . and that includes shipment."
2. Close on a trade: "If we can meet your deadline, do we have an agreement?"
3. Summarize, get agreement, and close:

Seller: "All right, we've agreed to . . . Did I leave anything out?"
Buyer: "No, that's it."
Seller: "Great, it looks like we have an agreement!"
(Shake hands).

❐ **214. Don't give the store away to close the deal.** Sellers mistakenly believe that by continuing to agree to last requests, the negotiation will end. All it leads to is a bad deal for the seller.

Weak:

Buyer: ". . . and I want a hot line to your tech department at no charge."

Seller: "Okay."

Buyer: ". . . and an on-site inspection every quarter."

Seller: "Okay."

Buyer: ". . . and no charge for repairs."

Seller: "Okay."

Buyer: ". . . and . . ."

Better:

Buyer: ". . . and I want a hot line to your tech department at no charge."

Seller: "If I can arrange that, do we have an agreement?"

❐ **215. Always be the one to summarize an agreement.** To avoid any misunderstanding or embarrassment, summarize the agreement. Then, put it in writing.

NUMBER OF CHECKS
*(tips you are currently doing/using):*_____

❐ **39–43** = *Top Performer*

❐ **34–38** = *Above Average*

❐ **30–33** = *Average*

❐ **26–29** = *Fair*

❐ **Below 26** = *Poor*

NEGOTIATING POWER RANKING:_____

BUILDING RELATIONSHIPS

"I will pay more for the ability to get along with people than for any other ability."

—JOHN D. ROCKEFELLER

Early Contact with Buyers

☐ **216. Build credibility with clients in prospecting letters.** Include three to five testimonial letters from satisfied clients. *Write:* "P.S. The enclosed letters give you a sense of the value you could expect to receive from XYZ Company." The message the prospect gets is that you are legitimate and worth her time.

☐ **217. Little things mean a lot.** Spell names and titles correctly. Ms. Pat Birner, Executive Vice President, does not respond kindly to letters addressed to Mr. Pat Berner, Senior Vice President. If in doubt, call the secretary or company operator first.

Building Interpersonal Contact

☐ **218. Tune up your small-talk antennae.** Not everyone wants to talk about last night's game, what he did on the weekend, or how often he sails the boat that's in the picture you spot on his credenza. Before you chat, check your client's mood and proceed accordingly.

☐ **219. Ask clients what solving a problem or meeting an objective will mean to them personally.** Tip O'Neill, former Speaker of the House from Massachusetts, once said, "All politics is local." On some level, all business is *personal*. People have ambitions, fears, and hopes. Identify these and help clients achieve their personal goals as much as possible.

☐ **220. Use your buyers' jargon.** If your clients call rich people "High Net Worth Individuals," as they do in banking, then you call them that, too. If they refer to department stores as "Doors," as they do in the cosmetics industry, then you do, too. People like people who speak and understand their language.

☐ **221. Be a full-time listener.** Sometimes, clients *want* to talk about business. Sometimes they *need* to talk about nonbusiness issues. Be a good listener in **both** instances.

❐ **222. Think "we"; talk "we."** When you provide important products or services to a company, you come to identify with them on some level and they should see you, in a similar way, as part of the "family." So, instead of asking your clients, "How are you doing?" ask, "How are we doing?"

❐ **223. Better to underpromise and overdeliver than the other way around.** Expectations are everything. Don't give clients a reason to seek a new supplier.

❐ **224. Keep a diary on buyers.** Include important personal information they share with you: children's graduations, birth of a grandchild, family illness, vacation plans. Remember to ask about these people and events when you see or speak to them again. People feel good when you are thoughtful enough to remember what they said.

❐ **225. Help a client who is new to your town or city develop an initial support network.** Be willing to recommend schools, dry cleaners, barber shops, doctors, good shopping, a car dealer, etc.

❐ **226. Don't confuse business friendship with personal friendship.** If you become genuine personal friends with business contacts, that's fine. However, there's a fine line between the two. Respect it.

❐ **227. Send birthday cards only when you have a genuine personal friendship with your buyers.** Anything less and you're being presumptuous.

❐ **228. Reverse roles.** Think of a recent *positive* sales experience you had when you were the buyer (e.g., for a gift, a car, a house, an appliance, a broker). Write down how that salesperson made you feel and what he/she did to make you feel that way. Compare this list to what you do with your clients. Are you doing everything possible to make your clients feel the same way?

❐ **229. Do midyear reviews with clients.** Thank them for their business. Summarize for them the positive things your two firms have done together in the past six months. Tactfully remind them of any extras they've enjoyed; e.g., training at no charge. Ask them what they think you and your firm could be doing to improve service or offer by way of new products. This is not a hard-sell meeting but a true business-review meeting.

Business Courtesies

❐ **230. Send a thank-you note to people for their business.** Express excitement to be working with them. Emphasize that you will do everything possible to ensure success for all concerned. Good manners promote strong relationships.

❒ **231. Thank them again.** Send along a note of appreciation for the business after they start to use your product or service. Send another note, or take them to a thank-you lunch, at the conclusion of a project. People like to be appreciated.

❒ **232. Write a letter to key people on your buyer's support staff thanking them for their help in getting your project/program/system/business up and running.** The secretary, administrative assistant, research director all appreciate recognition. It pays to have people on *all* levels at an account think well of you.

❒ **233. Bring your boss to a "thank you" lunch.** People feel as important as they are treated. Let your customers know that you *and* your management appreciate their business.

❒ **234. Don't be a "love 'em and leave 'em" sales rep.** After the sale has been made, be visible for implementation. Make sure internal people are up to speed on any special client needs. Be available to the client for questions. Follow up at the appropriate time to see how things are going. Make your clients feel that they are the most important customers your firm has.

☐ **235. During the holiday season, remember your client's secretary.** Send something that reflects some thought: a book on a topic you know is of interest to him/her, flowers or a plant, a gift certificate to a good department store, etc. Bosses may decide contracts, but *secretaries* decide who gets through to the bosses.

Maintaining the Highest Professional Relationships

☐ **236. Keep your word.** If you say you will have something back to the client by the eighteenth, the nineteenth is too late. If you say you'll call at 10, 10:05 is too late. If the meeting starts at 9, arriving at 9:05 is too late. Trust is often won or lost through these little transgressions.

☐ **237. Be the first with good—and bad—news.** Never let a client hear about a problem from someone else first. Call immediately. Apologize. Explain what steps you are taking to fix the problem. Manage all your company's resources necessary to correct the problem as quickly and efficiently as possible. Double-check with the client afterwards to ensure the damage to your relationship has been repaired. Always be first with the good news as well. Your client will appreciate the bearer of good tidings.

☐ **238. Cross-train employees.** Invite your client's back-office people to spend a day with your back-office people so that, ultimately, all processing happens more quickly between the two firms. Depending on your business, look for opportunities to strengthen the bond between your two companies through your employees.

❐ **239. Periodically, check out the quality of your own company's customer service.** Call and pretend to be a customer. See how you are treated. Identify any problems and fix them ASAP—before your customers experience them.

❐ **240. Train your secretary** to handle client problems professionally, so that your clients know they are working with a strong team.

❐ **241. Never do anything unethical.** Lying, bribery, cutting side deals, or sharing proprietary information have no place in a professional business relationship. If in doubt, then you probably shouldn't do it.

Making It Fun to See You!

❐ **242. Be someone your buyers want to see.** Be upbeat, without being a Pollyanna. Bring in news of real value to your buyer. Allow your natural sense of humor to come through. Recommend an interesting new book. Bring hot coffee in winter and lemonade in the summer.

❒ **243. Be the "host with the most."** Buyers see salespeople all the time, but they rarely have time to meet their counterparts at other companies. Set up a simple lunch with two or three of your (noncompetitive) customers, the sole purpose of which is to relax and enjoy one another's company. They will have a good time, generally reinforce the value of your products or services to one another, and be really appreciative of your thoughtfulness in bringing them together.

❒ **244. Entertain imaginatively.** Instead of the usual restaurant business lunch, try afternoon tea (a leisurely alternative to the power lunch), lunch at the local museum or on a ferry, grab a hot dog and stroll through the park on a beautiful day, go for workouts or massages, get your tea leaves read, or attend a lecture on a timely topic. Make sure your plans are appropriate for the tastes of your client, but make it interesting, as well as smart, business to know you.

❒ **245. Send close clients postcards from exotic or unusual vacation spots.** Include a light, upbeat message. Say you'll call when you return.

Making Clients Feel Important

❒ **246. Quote clients in your company newsletter, or ask them to write an article for it.** Have it reprinted professionally, frame it, and send it to them with a thank-you note. Everyone likes to see his or her name in lights and, if not in lights, at least in print.

❐ 247. Sponsor a client conference or breakfast.
Bring in a prominent outside speaker. Demonstrate a new technology. Make working with your company a real added-value learning relationship for clients.

❐ 248. Invite a client to speak at a company sales meeting or luncheon.
The topic could be on an industry trend or on what makes a good salesperson. Give them a small token of your appreciation for taking the time to do this. Clients are flattered to be taken into the company's "family."

❐ 249. Ask a good client to pilot a new product or program at a substantially reduced rate.
Your client feels special that you selected him. He gets a bargain. You get a real time test. Everyone wins!

❐ 250. Ask your client's advice.
Perhaps you have a question about industry trends, or you're thinking of introducing a new service, or you want a reaction to a new promotional brochure. If clients become good business friends, they are flattered when you seek out the wisdom of their opinions.

Staying in Touch

☐ **251. Publish a client newsletter.** Give it an appropriate, catchy title: *The Ryan Record*; *Sixty Seconds from Sam*; *In-Touch*; *What's New!* Include industry news of value; a client success story; new product or service information; and something amusing, like a cartoon.

☐ **252. Don't let "squeaky wheel" customers ride over your best customers.** Spend as much time caring for good clients as you do tending to problem clients. Look for ways to improve customer service and provide additional problem-solving services. Otherwise, those good clients will look elsewhere for attention and become your next problem.

Seeding Future Relationships

☐ **253. Ask to be put on your buyers' internal mailing list for company newsletters and announcements.** These keep you up-to-date on executive moves, new-product information, and any other changes that could affect your business.

☐ **254. Cultivate tomorrow's decision makers today.** The assistant vice president you ignore today is next week's vice president. The nobodies you snubbed for the last three months change jobs and become somebodies at a new company. Decision makers are important to know, but so are influencers. Ignore them at your peril.

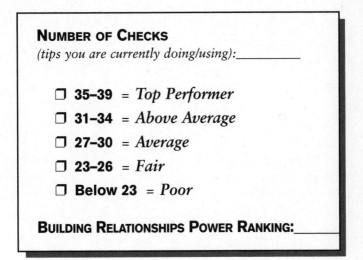

NUMBER OF CHECKS
*(tips you are currently doing/using):*_____

- ❐ **35–39** = *Top Performer*
- ❐ **31–34** = *Above Average*
- ❐ **27–30** = *Average*
- ❐ **23–26** = *Fair*
- ❐ **Below 23** = *Poor*

BUILDING RELATIONSHIPS POWER RANKING:_____

CREATIVE THINKING

"When the only tool you have is a hammer, you tend to treat everything as if it were a nail."

—ABRAHAM MASLOW,
psychologist

Getting a Creative Outlook

☐ **255. Believe you are creative.** You may never be Jack Nicklaus, Michael Jordan, or Monica Seles, but you can still play—and enjoy—a decent game of golf, basketball, or tennis. Likewise, you don't have to be Einstein or Picasso to participate in the creative process.

☐ **256. Think positively!** Creative people always believe there's a solution to a problem. They may not have the solution at a given moment, but they know it's there, waiting to be discovered.

☐ **257. Get rid of fear.** The biggest block to being creative is fear of looking stupid or fear of appearing different. Much fearfulness has its roots in early school experiences, where kids who were different were often seen as "weirdos" or "nerds." Look around you. Many of those "nerds" from yesterday are today's business successes.

☐ **258. Be open to challenging old thinking.** Routine and the unwillingness to experiment with new ways of thinking are major blocks to thinking. The worst offenders are sometimes successful salespeople, who rely on past behaviors for future success. Remember the old saying *"One way you know you're an old dog is when you stop learning new tricks."*

☐ **259. Adopt a problem-solving attitude.** Observe the problems begging for creative solutions all around us, at home, and in the different environments in which we find ourselves: airports, supermarkets, highways, schools, beaches, movie lines, etc. Imagine as many ways as possible to solve these problems.

☐ **260. Allow yourself to be childlike.** The most creative people are children. Give them a set of blocks and they create whole worlds without any concern for what other people might think: they create cities, fortresses, treasure islands, castles. Be playful, without self-consciousness, and without caring a fig what others think of your ideas.

Enhancing Creative Thinking Skills

☐ **261. Practice "mental pinball."** Strong creative thinkers are highly *associative*. They let their ideas loose to bounce around like balls in a pinball machine. This random thinking process leads suddenly (aha!) to a solution. Exercise: Free-associate twenty items or thoughts from a single word. Repeat with a new word and increase the number: thirty, forty, fifty, etc. For example: free-associate around the color *red*: blood, heart, love, lovers, roses, thorns, pain, hospital, doctors, white coats, winter, etc.

☐ **262.** *"An idea is a feat of association."*

—ROBERT FROST

☐ **263. Spend some time with children—yours or borrowed ones, like neighbors' kids, nieces, or nephews.** Children help rediscover the spontaneous, playful part of yourself, which is so important to creative thinking.

☐ **264. Visit a toy store.** It will elevate your mood, relieve stress, and help in creative thinking. (Just avoid the Christmas crush!)

☐ **265. Break routine patterns.** Creative thinkers see and do things differently. Start to break your own patterns. Wear red, if you never wear red. Say hello to people in elevators. Browse in a new section of the bookstore. Start a meal with dessert. Walk home on the other side of the street.

☐ **266. Relax your way to a new idea.** Trying to force an idea is like trying to force love between two people: the time pressure rarely produces the desired result. While ideas sometimes come quickly, like love at first sight, those times are the exceptions. One creative thinking technique is to put your problem aside for a few days. The solution often comes to you while you are doing something unrelated, like walking, shaving, exercising, playing with the kids.

☐ **267. Create the environment that brings out <u>your</u> best thinking.** Like athletes who psychologically feel and play better when they wear the same winning socks for every game, create your own "socks" environment where ideas can happen: sitting on a soft couch? wearing casual clothes? listening to music?

☐ **268. Warm up your creative thinking "muscles."** Exercise: Take two unrelated objects and force as many comparisons between them as possible. Example: A flower and an egg. Both have color. Both have two parts to them. Both will die without being cared for. Both enhance our lives: one with beauty, the other with nourishment. Both frequently come in quantity: a bouquet of flowers, a carton of eggs. Your turn: 1. an elephant and an emerald 2. an orchestra and your job.

☐ **269. Work in short time-frames:** sixty to ninety minutes. Then, take a break. Walk around. Eat something. Get some fresh air. Come back to the problem refreshed and ready to go again.

Group Brainstorming

☐ **270. Buddy up for brainstorming.** Trying to solve a thorny problem by yourself is stressful and frustrating. Use the wisdom and imagination of your colleagues in a brainstorming session. You'll get more done in less time with better results—and have more fun in the process.

☐ **271. Laughter and fun feed the creative process.** You generate more and better ideas in the right frame of mind. In a group session, have fun "stuff" on the tables: candy you ate as children, colored crayons for writing. Give silly prizes for the most bizarre or funniest idea, etc.

"If you lose the power to laugh, you lose the power to think."

—CLARENCE DARROW

❑ **272. For quality, go for quantity.** You take hundreds of pictures at a wedding to get a handful of really good photos. When you need to solve a problem, generate as many ideas as possible, good, bad, and indifferent ones, to find one that really pays off. The best solutions often come from the most outrageous ideas. Who would have thought people would willingly walk around with earphones in their ears?

❑ **273. Beware the great sales strength that becomes a great weakness.** Good salespeople pride themselves on being able to move a sale to closure as expeditiously as possible. That drive to close backfires creatively. The quick closer settles for the first or second idea rather than taking the time to generate many ideas, which usually leads to a better idea.

❑ **274. Be positive, be upbeat, and you'll be creative!** Expressions like "It won't work," "We tried that before," or "That's a dumb idea" kill the creative thinking process quicker than a fire hose extinguishes a campfire. Replace these negative responses with "How can we build on that?" or "Let's look at the best parts of that idea."

❑ **275. Hitchhike onto each other's ideas.** An unlikely idea often triggers the thinking that leads to the terrific idea. You'll get to your destination (the new idea) faster when you *build* on each other's ideas in a brainstorming session.

☐ **276. Separate idea generation from idea evaluation.** Get all your ideas out on the table first. Then, put on your "judging hat" and decide which ones you want to use.

Creative Thinking Exercises

☐ **277. Get outside <u>your</u> perspective to get inside a new idea.** Imagine how three very different famous celebrities or historical figures would solve your problem. For example: the pope, Bill Gates, and Madonna.

☐ **278. Look for your solution in other worlds (e.g., nature, music, sports) or in other industries (e.g., transportation, investing).** For example, airlines use frequent-flier miles to increase customer travel and loyalty. Can you offer points, credits, bonuses to your customers in return for increased business?

☐ **279. Play "What If?"** What if you changed a factor in the problem? Ask, "What can I substitute? modify? expand? shrink? add? subtract? adapt? put to another use? reverse?" Example:

Problem: To get in to see a key decision maker.

Solution: Reverse your premise: "What if I could get her to want to see me."

Ideas: Invite her to an important luncheon . . . Arrange a lunch with one of her peers at another company whom she would want to meet . . . Send her one movie theater coupon and tell her she gets a second one when we meet. "What if?s" have high payoffs.

☐ **280. Think of the worst possible idea.** It often leads to a workable idea.

Problem: A colleague who talks too much at client team meetings.

Worst idea: Sew his mouth up!

Aha!: Make him the official note taker of everything the team discusses, so that most of his time will be spent writing and he won't have the opportunity to talk.

☐ **281. You only have to be right once.** Creative problem solving often leads you to several dead ends until you finally find the right idea. Being wrong many times is part of the process.

Creativity in the Office

☐ **282. Set up three-person Idea Teams.** Meet weekly for the express purpose of brainstorming solutions to one another's sticky sales problems. Change at least one person on the team every month to keep the creative energy and output fresh.

☐ **283. Install an office "Weekly Idea Box."** Ideas can be for improving customer service, increasing business, saving money, cutting costs, or for new products, or new ways to get in to see people. Give fun prizes for the best ideas. Give meaningful prizes for the ideas that get used.

☐ **284. At the beginning of sales meetings ask people to share one new, non–sales related fact or idea.** For example, Einstein failed math. Cheetahs can go from zero to forty-five miles per hour in three seconds, reaching a speed of seventy miles per hour, but can only sustain that in one minute spurts before they exhaust themselves. It takes them twenty minutes to recover.

Being on the lookout for bits and pieces of information from other fields forces people out of their patterned thinking.

☐ **285. Learn more about creative thinking.** Information on creative thinking is as close as your nearest bookstore. *Thinkertoys,* by Michael Michalko, and *99% Inspiration,* by Bryan W. Mattimore, are just two of many excellent books published on this subject. (If you're interested in a creative thinking seminar for your sales staff, contact me at 212 876-1875.)

❐ **286.** *"Imagination is more important than knowledge."*

—ALBERT EINSTEIN

NUMBER OF CHECKS
*(tips you are currently doing/using):*_____

❐ **29–32** = *Top Performer*

❐ **26–28** = *Above Average*

❐ **23–25** = *Average*

❐ **19–22** = *Fair*

❐ **Below 19** = *Poor*

CREATIVE THINKING POWER RANKING:_____

WORKING SMART

Luck is preparation meeting opportunity.

Reaching Goals

☐ **287. Work with goals.** If you don't know where you're going, you're likely to wind up nowhere. Goals drive activity and give direction to our lives. People with goals have a sense of purpose and an inner sense of confidence. Goals are the discipline that enables us to grow and enjoy life. Achieving them feels good and expands us as human beings. That is true in both personal and business life.

☐ **288. Make goals specific, realistic, and written out.** In business, instead of saying "I'm going to increase my prospecting," say "I'm going to make twenty additional new business calls a month." In your family life, instead of saying "I'm going to spend more time with my children," say, "I'm going to become a soccer coach or a den mother."

❑ 289. Put deadlines on your goals. Jazz great Duke Ellington declared, "Without a deadline, baby, I wouldn't do nothing." Instead of saying "I want to be a sales manager someday," say, "I want to be a sales manager *by the time I am thirty*." Replace "I want to spend more time with my spouse" with "My spouse and I are going to get a weekend away once a month *starting this month*."

❑ 290. Meet aggressive goals by stretching them 50 to 100 percent. If, for example, your goal is to have twenty face-to-face sales calls in a week, stretch it to forty. Then, list all the things you would do to meet that aggressive target. The simple act of writing down your strategies will inevitably result in several new ideas that will help you reach your initial goal with ease—and give you a treasure trove of ideas to propel you to the next level.

❑ 291. Add "fuel" to your goals: create written action steps. If you've decided to become a sales manager by the time you're thirty, your list of action steps might include: joining professional organizations, volunteering for high-visibility jobs in the company, attending a course to improve knowledge and skills, networking with key people in the company, writing articles for industry media, etc. If you want a monthly weekend away with your spouse, your list of action steps might include finding a regular baby-sitter, selecting dates, deciding where to go, sending for brochures, etc.

☐ **292. Transfer action steps to your calendar.**
Check your list of action steps regularly (weekly, monthly) and work them into your calendar, so that they become part of your daily "To do" lists. Very shortly, you will have the satisfaction of seeing yourself achieve the goals you wanted. Then, start the process all over again!

☐ **293. Don't confuse activity with productivity.** Always ask yourself, "Is this the best use of my time right now?" If the answer is "No," then stop what you are doing and start working on what is the best use of your time right then.

Getting Organized

☐ **294. Put your "mind-in-the-drawer" for perfect follow-up.** Needed: one *daily* and one *monthly* accordion envelope business sorter file. What needs to get done at a later day this month gets filed in the right date in the *Daily* thirty-one-day file. What needs to get done in a future month is put in the right slot in the *Monthly* file. At the beginning of a month, you transfer the contents of the Monthly file into appropriate dates in the Daily file. Nothing gets lost. Include business, personal, and family items, so that *everything* important in your life gets done.

☐ **295. Clean up your desk at the end of the day and prepare for the next day's activities.** A few minutes devoted to straightening up at the end of the day gives you a sense of closure and lets you start the next day fresh and raring to go!

❐ **296. If you have something important to do, <u>schedule</u> it.** "When I find the time, I'll do it," are the famous last words of many busy people. No one ever finds extra time. You need to block out the time to finish that proposal, develop a new idea, or complete an important research project. Keep that time protected just as you would if it were a meeting with a client. In this case, what more important client do you have than yourself?

❐ **297. Work in concentrated time blocks.** Don't jump from activity to activity. The most efficient and productive way to work is in dedicated time blocks. Spend an uninterrupted hour returning phone calls; an uninterrupted thirty minutes to complete that special letter; an uninterrupted hour working on phase one of a big project. Protect your time and you'll accomplish your important work.

Time-Savers

❐ **298. Write the notes of your follow-up telephone conversation on the letter that you sent to that prospect.** If follow-up is required, slip the letter with the notes on it into your future file. This cuts down on the amount of paper you use and ensures that all the key information stays together.

☐ **299. How to help others without giving up your time.** As a successful salesperson, you are likely to get calls from advice seekers or job hunters requesting a breakfast, lunch, or office appointment to discuss their career or business problems. Regretfully state that your calendar is jammed up, but that you'd be happy to give them a few minutes of your best thinking on the phone right then. Be as genuinely helpful as you can. Then, wish them luck, hang up, and get back to your work.

☐ **300. Get lost!** People can't interrupt you if they can't find you. When you need time to think, to write a proposal, to develop an account strategy, find a quiet place to do it *away* from the office.

☐ **301. Use your calendar for fire-fighting time.** Leave an hour a day free in your schedule for all the unexpected problems that can—and will—pop up.

☐ **302. Movable to-do lists.** If you use a paper calendar (as opposed to an electronic one) write out your to-do list on a large Post-It that you can move from page to page until your list is completed. You won't have to write up a

new list every day even though you'll be adding to it as
you finish tasks.

❑ **303. Color it!** Identify key items by color coding. This
simple technique will drive your choice of activities and
keep you focused on the most important things first. On a
desk of all white paper, important papers get lost among
unimportant papers. Use colored folders to indicate high-
priority items; e.g., red for "Do Now," blue for "The
Boss," yellow for "Urgent Problems," or put a red-colored
dot on papers that need attention that day. Color attracts
the eye.

❑ **304. Avoid telephone tag.** Set up your next appointment at the end of the present meeting.

Buyer: "Send me that information."
Weak:
Seller: "Great. I'll send you that material and then call
   you."
Better:
Seller: "Great. I'll send you that material. *Let's set up a
   meeting now to review it, while we both have our cal-
   endars. How's the twelfth at nine o'clock?*"

Smart Selling

☐ **305. Back to basics.** Have an objective for every call. Identify the specific, time-related action step the buyer should take to indicate your objective has been achieved. Example: *Objective*—to establish a relationship with a new account. *Action Step*—Client agrees to introduce me to the next management level within the next two weeks.

☐ **306. Know Your Customer.** Buyers respect, and are willing to talk to, salespeople who understand them and their business. You can find this information in trade media, from your internal sources, from colleagues, on the Internet (visit their Web site), in annual reports, and from *buyers'* customers.

☐ **307. Get smart fast about a new industry/company.** In addition to on-line information services:

1. Ask a securities broker to send you his firm's latest research report on that industry.
2. Buy the annual industry review issues published by the leading business magazines in January of each year. In a few paragraphs, you get a solid overview of the dynamics facing that industry and the major players in it.

❐ **308. Call for recruitment brochures.** Since the goal of a recruitment brochure is to attract the best and brightest to work at their firms, they usually include a good breakdown of departments and often include senior management's names and job titles. They also give you a good feel for the company's view of itself. Information is power, and recruitment brochures give you an additional handle on prospects.

❐ **309. Spend time with your customer's customers.** Do you sell to the computer industry? Drop in on a computer store, talk to the salespeople and ask what's moving, what's not. Do you sell to the banking industry? Attempt to open an account at a couple of banks and see how you're treated. You can never have too many perspectives on your customers.

❐ **310. Read your customers' trade press.** Become as familiar with their industry trends, jargon, and personalities as you are with your own. Customers respect people who know and understand their business.

❐ **311. Talk to cabdrivers.** In many cities, particularly the smaller ones, when you're going from the airport to the city, strike up a conversation to get the latest on the local business scene. Cabdrivers know how the economy is really doing, since their business feels its effects first. They often know things about major corporations in town because of things they hear in the cab and friends and relatives who work at these companies. And, if they can't help, you can always talk politics (!).

☐ **312. Get an annual report card.** Create a comprehensive performance survey on you, your products, and your company. Give it to a cross-section of your clients to be filled out anonymously and sent back in preaddressed, prestamped envelopes. Do this annually to monitor the satisfaction levels your clients have with you and your company. Then, act on their feedback.

☐ **313. Trade show tip.** The first evening of any conference or convention is usually an arrival day with nothing planned, so it's a perfect time to invite a key client or prospect out for dinner or to host a small cocktail party for a special group.

Working Smart Inside Your Company

☐ **314. Treat your secretary/assistant like your business partner.** In addition to sharing the names, titles, and relationships of the key players at your accounts, keep your secretary apprised of your account strategies, company news, and your general business thinking. As your front line to the world, your secretary will be better able to help you reach your bottom-line goals with the company.

❒ 315. Treat the personnel in internal support departments like clients. Get to know them personally. Visit them in *their* offices. Be respectful of their time. Thank them for getting a job done on time. Get to be #1 on their hit parade, so that you become #1 on their priority list.

Getting New Business

❒ 316. Make friends with secretaries when you prospect. When your prospect is unavailable, ask, "Is this Ms. Prospect's assistant?" When he/she answers "Yes," say, "Good!" Then (1) state your name and company, (2) ask his/her name, (3) state the reason you are calling, and (4) ask when he/she suggests you call again. Then, when you call, greet her/him as a friend. This often gets you through to your prospect more quickly.

❒ 317. Get testimonial letters. When clients say how pleased they are with your products or services, ask them if they would put those sentiments into a brief fan letter. Tell them that references are always requested in your business and rather than bother clients with phone calls, it's much more efficient to be able to show these letters. Most clients will be happy to write these letters for you.

❒ 318. Ask for referrals. When clients tell you what a great job your product or service is doing for them, ask them for the names of two people they know, in similar positions, who might use your products or services.

☐ **319. Be visible in your industry.** Attend trade shows. Write a newsletter. Chair an association committee. Run for an association office. Sponsor a charitable event. Speak on a panel. Be someone people know and respect as a committed industry supporter and expert.

Personal Image

☐ **320. Develop a signature style.** Do you always wear a beautiful scarf or a distinctive tie? Do you send out off-beat articles for fun or general interest? Do you follow up with handwritten, rather than printed, notes? Do you find unusual places to take clients for lunch? Whatever it is, stand out (tastefully) from the crowd.

☐ **321. Be unpredictable in a positive way.** Call clients for non-sales reasons. Congratulate them when their company appears in the newspaper. Ask their opinion about breaking industry developments. Share a story of interest. Remind them of an upcoming conference. Inquire about a major event in their lives; e.g., a child's wedding. Clients will take your calls more often if they don't think you're always calling to sell them something.

☐ **322. Send greeting cards at unexpected times.**
Everyone sends season's greetings cards in December,
when they are sure to get lost in the flood of good wishes
most clients receive then. You may feel compelled to do
that, but when you send New Year's greeting cards and
mail them to arrive in the first week of January, you and
your card will stand out. And, you will reach people when
they're thinking about business.

Professional Development

☐ **323.** *"I am always learning."*

—MICHELANGELO

Attend sales and business seminars, listen to tapes, read
leading business publications, attend trade shows. Be on
the cutting edge of your business.

☐ **324. Work for smart people.** If you are not learning
from your boss, or from colleagues, it's time to change
jobs or seek a different position in your company.

☐ **325. Have a personal advisory board.** Establish a
circle of industry experts you can call periodically. Ask
them about the implications of new trends, new technolo-
gies, changes in regulations, mergers, changes in the business, and the problems and challenges they see both short-
and long-term for the industry. Be a pro-active, rather than
a re-active, salesperson.

❐ **326. Start a Sales Book Club.** It's impossible to read all the latest books on selling and business. Meet once a month with colleagues and have each person report the highlights of a book he/she has read. In one hour, you'll walk away with new money-making ideas and reinforce your connection with business colleagues.

Personal Well-Being

❐ **327. High standards? Yes. Perfectionism? No.** People who aim to be perfect are constantly frustrated, become stressed out in the process, and are destined to fail. People who do the best they can generally come out on top and achieve success with far less stress. Remember, Babe Ruth held records for the most home runs *and* the most strikeouts.

❐ **328. Step out of your comfort zone periodically.** Go on a mountain hiking trip. Shoot the rapids. Learn to ski, sail, or tap dance. Put yourself in a totally different environment and experience the challenge of learning something new. You'll feel renewed, rejuvenated, reenergized, and ready to reach even greater heights when you return to work.

❐ **329. Even express trains make some local stops.** Recognize when your "gung-ho, take no prisoners, no-mountain-too-high" energy train needs to pause to rejuvenate, to relax, to give attention to the other important parts and people in your life. Get away for the weekend. Spend time with friends or relatives you haven't seen for a while. Listen to music, go to a museum, attend a sports event, read a book. Go to the gym, take a run in the park, spend a weekend morning at a spa. Whatever you choose, short periodic breaks will lead to even greater sales success for you.

☐ **330. Do a work-life balance check.** At least once a year (on your birthday?), make a list of the important areas of your life: personal relationships, family, career, hobbies, community, spiritual, or other. Rate your satisfaction in each on a scale of, say, 1 to 7. Devise specific plans to increase those low numbers. Have you neglected your friends? Invite them to dinner or to a sporting event. Have you lost your sense of physical fitness? Get up an hour earlier three times a week and run. Are you feeling guilty about your lack of charity work? Volunteer, even if only for an hour a week. Once scheduled, keep that time sacred.

☐ **331. Never lose your sense of humor.** While political, ethnic, and religious jokes have no place in your work life, natural humor is very human and quite acceptable. A shared spontaneous laugh instantly brings people closer together. Remember, "The shortest distance between two people is a smile" (*Victor Borge*).

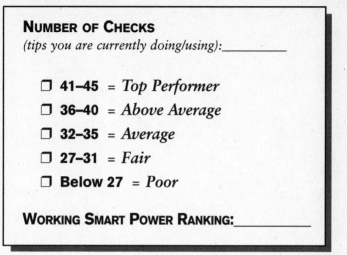

NUMBER OF CHECKS
*(tips you are currently doing/using):*_____

☐ **41–45** = *Top Performer*
☐ **36–40** = *Above Average*
☐ **32–35** = *Average*
☐ **27–31** = *Fair*
☐ **Below 27** = *Poor*

WORKING SMART POWER RANKING:_____

ATTITUDE AND MOTIVATION

"Ability is what you're capable of doing. Motivation determines what you do. Attitude determines how well you do it."

—LOU HOLTZ,
legendary Notre Dame
football coach

Staying Upbeat and On Track

❒ **332. Create a personal mission statement.** Frame it. Post it where you can see it every day. Live it. Sample: "My mission is (1) to help my clients build their business and (2) to provide a comfortable life for my family and myself. I strive to be professional and ethical at all times. I learn from adversity and aim to be the best that I can be. It's important that my clients respect me and that we all have fun and grow in the work we do together."

❒ **333. The difference between ordinary and extraordinary is that <u>extra</u>.** Can you make one more call?

write one more letter? see one more person? What little *extra* can you do today?

□ 334. Where you have a choice, seek out positive, supportive people: people who appreciate you, who can teach you something, who make you laugh, who energize you, who love you. Avoid everyone else.

□ 335. Winners keep their eye on the outcome, not the process. If you have a task that you are procrastinating about doing—a long proposal to write, a list of prospects to call—*imagine* how you will feel once it is done. *Think* of the time it will free up for you. *Feel* the relief of having it done.

□ 336. Learn from the past. Focus on the future. Achievers see mistakes—bad sales calls, lost sales, errors in judgment—as *opportunities* to review what they did and learn from the experience. When Thomas Edison was asked how he could persist in his experiments when he had failed over nine hundred times, he replied, "Don't be silly. I haven't failed. I now know 999 ways not to make incandescent light."

□ 337. Keep a file of testimonial letters from satisfied clients. On days when no one seems to be buying, reread the letters. Let them raise your spirits by reminding you of the tremendous value your products and services really do provide to people.

□ **338. Get past bad days: ask for a compliment.** Call up a close client, tell him you're having a terrible day, and ask him to tell you again why he likes your product or service. Let his glowing endorsements jump-start your (temporarily) stalled enthusiasm.

□ **339. Use a new goal to dig out of ruts.** Psychologists will tell you that the best way to get out of a slump is to **do** something.

□ **340. To feel up, act up.** It's hard to stay negative when you're acting positively. Put a twinkle in your eye, enthusiasm in your voice, and a spring in your step.

□ **341. To be positive, talk positively.** Do you talk about *problems* or *opportunities, can'ts* and *won'ts* or *can's* and *will's*? Do you ask *why?* or *why not?* Language shapes reality. Keep yours positive.

□ **342. It's hard to stay blue when you're blowing bubbles!** Keep fun stuff in your office: bubbles, chimes, a squeegee ball, cartoons.

❐ **343. If it isn't fun, make it fun! Have a good laugh every day!**

❐ **344. Reward yourself for small victories:** for making a record number of calls in a week; for getting out a record number of proposals in a short period of time; for getting through to a tough customer; for cracking a new account. Wins come in various shapes and sizes. Celebrate them all!

❐ **345. Exercise!** When you're physically fit and energetic, you tend to be psychologically fit and energetic as well.

❐ **346. Don't let age stop you.** George Burns won his first Oscar at eighty. Golda Meir was seventy-one when she became prime minister of Israel. Michelangelo was seventy-one when he painted the Sistine Chapel. Go for it!

❐ **347. Help someone.** We never feel so satisfied as when we see the gratitude on the face of someone we've helped. Volunteer for your favorite charity. Tutor a student. Do community work. People who do good feel good.

❑ **348. Frame a meaningful motivational or inspirational quote and keep it visible in your office at all times** (or post it on your computer as a screen-saver!).

Words to Inspire

❑ **349.** *"Always be a first-rate version of yourself, instead of a second-rate version of somebody else."*
—JUDY GARLAND

❑ **350.** *"How many cares one loses when one decides not to be something, but* someone.*"*
—COCO CHANEL

❑ **351.** *"If you think you can, or, if you think you can't, you're probably right."*
—HENRY FORD

❑ **352.** *"Nobody can make you feel inferior without your consent."*
—ELEANOR ROOSEVELT

❑ **353.** *"Take your work, not yourself, seriously."*
—ANONYMOUS

☐ **354.** *"Nothing great was ever accomplished without enthusiasm."*

—RALPH WALDO EMERSON

☐ **355.** *"Good enough never is."*

—DEBBI FIELDS, founder, Mrs. Field's Cookies

Work

☐ **356.** *"I do not know how to get to the top without hard work. That is the recipe. It will not always get you to the top, but should get you pretty near."*

—MARGARET THATCHER

☐ **357.** *". . . as one goes through life one learns that if you don't paddle your own canoe, you don't move."*

—KATHARINE HEPBURN

☐ **358.** *"Everything comes to him who hustles while he waits."*

—THOMAS EDISON

☐ **359.** *"Even if you're on the right track, if you just sit there you're going to get hit."*

—WILL ROGERS

Persistence

☐ **360.** *"Never, never, never, never, never give up."*

—WINSTON CHURCHILL

Hard Times

☐ **361.** *"The way I see it, if you want the rainbow, you gotta put up with the rain."*

—DOLLY PARTON

☐ **362.** *"When the world gives you lemons, make lemonade."*

—ANONYMOUS

Risk

☐ **363.** *"If you never fail, you aren't taking enough risks."*

—ANONYMOUS

☐ **364.** *"You miss 100 percent of the shots you never take."*

—WAYNE GRETZKY

☐ **365.** *"Life is an adventure, or it's nothing."*

—HELEN KELLER

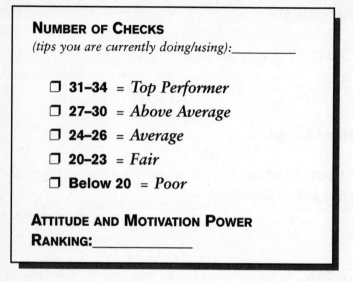

NUMBER OF CHECKS
*(tips you are currently doing/using):*_____

☐ **31–34** = *Top Performer*

☐ **27–30** = *Above Average*

☐ **24–26** = *Average*

☐ **20–23** = *Fair*

☐ **Below 20** = *Poor*

**ATTITUDE AND MOTIVATION POWER
RANKING:**_____

Measure Your Selling Power

1. Write the performance rankings you scored on the last page of each of the ten chapters in this book in the spaces below. (Top Performer, Above Average, Average, Fair, Poor)

_____ PROBING (Pro)

_____ LISTENING (Lis)

_____ PRESENTING (Pre)

_____ HANDLING OBJECTIONS (HO)

_____ CLOSING AND FOLLOW-THROUGH (Clo/FT)

_____ NEGOTIATING (Neg)

_____ WORKING SMART (WS)

_____ BUILDING RELATIONSHIPS (BR)

_____ CREATIVE THINKING (CT)

_____ ATTITUDE AND MOTIVATION (Att/Mo)

2. Plot these rankings on the Profile below.
3. Connect the dots. The lines give you your Selling Power Profile.

Sample:

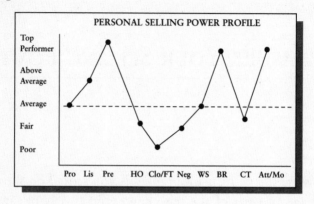

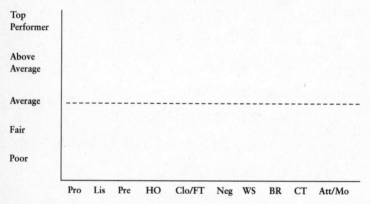

4. How to interpret your profile:

   Success in selling is only as strong as your performance in each phase of the sales cycle. A weakness in one area tends to cause sales problems in other areas. For example, weak probing skills and strategies get you inadequate information, which is likely to result in a presentation that is off the mark, which then provokes lots of objections from the buyer, which makes it impossible to close, which hurts the buyer-seller relationship, which leads to more time away from other business as you try for the business again, which increases stress, which dulls a positive attitude, etc.

To even out your scores at the highest possible levels:

A. Congratulate yourself on the strengths reflected in your higher rankings. Work on the tips you marked with an **X** in those chapters to further capitalize on these strengths.

B. Work on the areas reflected in the lower rankings. Return to those chapters and practice the tips in them that you originally marked with an **X**.

C. After a few weeks of working on these skills, score yourself again in each section to evaluate your progress.

To share your selling tips, or, for further information on Anne Miller's sales and communications speeches, seminars, and audiotapes,

call (212) 876-1875
e-mail: amspeak@aol.com
or, write:

Anne Miller
Chiron Associates, Inc.
Box 624
New York, NY 10163

INDEX

Action
  act now/later language
    clues, 20-21
  prompting from buyer, 8-9
Analogies
  key numbers, use of, 30
  in presentations, 30
Anger, and objections, 46-47
Annual report card, 115
Anxiety, and presentations,
  26, 27
Associative thinking, as
  creative thinking, 98

Birthday cards, to buyers, 88
Brainstorming, 101-103

Caring, importance of, 2-3
Closing
  attitude for, 56
  on buyer's question, 61
  follow-through, 64-65
  helping clients decide, 61
  lost business, learning
    about, 66-67
  meaning of, 55
  multi-buyer sale, 65-66
  of negotiation, 83-84
  on an objection, 60
  and procrastinating clients,
    62
  request for business, 59
  simple closing, 57

and spinning-wheel
  syndrome, 63
stopping selling, 58
with testimonials, 62
timing for, 56-57
waiter strategy, 63
working together plan, 64
Collaboration, and
  negotiation, 76
Color coding, high-priority
  items, 112
Committees, multi-buyer sale,
  65-66
Commodity tactic, 81
Competition, comparing
  products/services, 31-32
Contacting clients, comfort
  zones, 64-65
Courtesy
  being available, 89
  and client's secretary, 90
  thank-you lunch, 89
  thank-you notes, 88-89
Creative thinking
  associative thinking, 98
  brainstorming, 101-103
  breaking old patterns,
    99-100
  challenge old thinking, 97
  and childlike approach, 97
  environment for, 100
  exercises for, 99, 100-101,
    103-104

Creative thinking (*cont.*)
  forcing ideas, avoiding, 100
  idea teams in office,
      104-105
  information sources on,
      105-106
  and positive thinking, 97
  problem solving, 97
  seminar for, 106
  short-time frames for, 101
  weekly idea box, 105

Deadlines, for goals, 108
Decision making, on balance
    thinking, 61
Desk, daily clean-up, 109-110
Diary, on buyers, 87

Emotions
  and listening, 14, 19
  and objections, 46-47
Energy level, and
    presentations, 32
Entertaining clients, 89, 92,
    93
Exercise, 126
Eye contact, and listening,
    17-18

Fear, as thought blocker, 97
Flinch tactic, 81-82
Friendship, business versus
    personal, 87

Goals
  deadlines for, 108
  importance of, 107
  making specific, 107

and organization, 109-110
  stretching goals, 108
  time factors, 109
  written action steps for,
      108-109
Greeting cards, 118
Group brainstorming, 101-
    103
Guidelines pressure tactics, 79

Handouts, during
    presentations, 36
High-payoff questions, 7-8
Humor
  and objections, 41-42
  sense of humor, importance
      of, 120

"I'll think about it" objection,
    52-54
Image, signature style, 117
Information
  customers' trade press, 114
  new industry information,
      113
  recruitment brochures, 114

Jargon, use of, 86

Listening
  basic guidelines for, 13-15
  for buyer's priorities, 20
  and clarification, 18
  for client expectations, 21
  confirming phrases, 16, 17
  for contradictions, 18
  cues for formality/
      informality, 14

and emotions/opinions, 14, 19

encouraging listening, 15

for extreme reactions, 19

and eye contact, 17-18

versus hearing, 13

in the moment listening, 15

and relationship building, 86-87

summarizing information, 16-17

for tone of voice, 19

Midyear reviews, 88

Mini-presentations, 37-38

Mission statement, personal mission statement, 123

Mistakes, learning from past, 124

Motivation
personal mission statement, 123

reading positive testimonial letters, 125

rewarding self, 126

selling stars group, 124

and supportive people, 124

thinking about outcome, 124

Multi-buyer sale, closing, 65-66

Negotiation
agreement signals, 83

closing of, 83-84

and collaboration, 76

general guidelines, 69-70

interests versus demands, 73-74

justifying term, 76-77

and knowledge of seller, 70

mental readiness for, 72-73

one-issue negotiation, 74

opening discussion, 73-75

planning, 70-72

pressure tactics, types of, 78-82

price demands, 74-75, 76-77

raising stakes, 77

summarizing agreement, 82, 84

trade, 77

New business
from referrals, 116-117

testimonial letters to prospects, 116

Newsletter, client newsletter, 94

Nibble tactic, 82

Nonresponsive buyer, 50-52
seller handling of, 50-52

Note-taking, 4-5
confidential information, avoiding, 5

four-quarter page method, 5

Objections
acknowledging phrases, 43-44

anticipation of, 40

arguing, avoiding, 42

basic guidelines, 39-40

closing on objection, 60

Objections (*cont.*)
  depersonalizing objections, 39
  early objections, 40-41
  and emotions, 46-47
  humor, use of, 41-42
  "I'll think about it" objection, 52-54
  information-driven objections, 45-46
  killer phrase for seller, 44
  no-need objections, 50
  and nonresponsive buyer, 50-52
  phrases to avoid, 44
  post-objection check, 45
  price objections, 47-49
  probing of, 42-43
  using as selling point, 44-45
Opinions, and listening, 14
Organization
  color coding key items, 112
  daily desk clean-up, 109-110
  daily/monthly files, 109
  filing notes from conversations, 110-111
  and goals, 109-110
  scheduling extra time, 110
Organization chart, of decision-makers, 9

Perfectionism, 119
Personal advisory board, 118
Personal mission statement, 123

Phone appointments, setting up, 112
Positive impression, early in meeting, 3-4
Positive talk, 125
Positive thinking, 97
Presentations
  analogies, use of, 30
  and anxiety, 26, 27
  benefits for buyer, phrases for, 29
  body, use of, 32
  buyer as center of attention, 34
  and buyer's situation, 28
  conclusion of, 33-34
  and energy level, 32
  handouts, 36
  involvement of buyers, in, 30
  jokes, avoiding, 36-37
  mental preparation, 26-27
  mini-presentations, 37-38
  objections during, 28
  pausing, 33
  preparation for, 23-26
  questions during, 28
  script, use of, 27
  selling points, reinforcement of, 30
  success stories during, 29-30
  succinctness, 35
  tough questions, responding to, 35-36
  transitional phrases, 24
  visual aids, 24-25, 33

Pressure tactics, during negotiation, 78-82
Price
    negotiation of, 74-75, 76-77
    price objections, 47-49
    price tactics, 80
Probing
    budget question, 9
    client wish list, 10
    concluding session, 11-12
    conversational approach, 6-7
    high-payoff questions, 7-8
    lead-in phrases, 6
    of mindset, 1-2
    note-taking during, 4-5
    now questions, 8
    opening for, 3-4
    preparation of questions, 2-3
    guidelines for, 5-7
    scale question, 52-53
    testing client's thinking, 10-11
    tough questions, cushions for, 6
Problem solving, creative thinking, 97
Procrastinating clients, and closing, 62
Productivity, versus activity, 109
Professional development
    personal advisory board, 118
    sales book club, 119
    seminars, 118

Questions for buyer. See Probing
Quotes, in presentations, 24

Recruitment brochures, 114
Referrals, new business from, 116-117
Relationship building
    and accessibility to client, 89
    and buyer's jargon, 86
    client importance, activities for, 92-93
    client newsletter, 94
    cross-training client staff, 90-91
    and early contact, 85
    entertaining, 89, 92, 93
    for future relationships, 94-95
    handling good/bad news, 90
    improving customer service, 94
    and listening, 86-87
    and personal information on buyers, 87
    reversing roles, 88
    thank-you lunch, 89
    thank-you notes, 88-89
    unethical behavior, avoiding, 91
    "we," use of word, 87
Relaxation, 119-120
    exercise, 126
    work-life balance check, 120
Risk threshold, of buyer, 20

Role reversals
  and objections, 52
  and relationship building,
    88
Rule of Three, 34

Sales book club, 119
Scale question, 52-53
Schedule. *See* Time factors
Secretary
  as business partner, 115
  clients', 65, 90
Seminars, professional
    development, 118
Silence pressure, 80
Spinning-wheel syndrome,
    and closing, 63
Storyboard, preparation for
    presentations, 23
Suggestion box, 105
Summarizing, during
    negotiation, 82, 84
Supportive people, and
    motivation, 124

Terms of sale, negotiation of,
    76-77
Testimonials
  closing with, 62
  letters to new business
    prospects, 116
Thank-you lunch, 89
Thank-you notes, 88-89

Time factors
  goals, 109
  setting up phone
    appointments, 112
  time blocks for working,
    110
  time for closing, 56-57
  timing and helping others,
    111
  to-do lists, 111-112
  working away from office,
    111
Time tactic, 81
To-do lists, 111-112
Tone of voice, listening for,
    19
Trade shows, 115
Transitional phrases,
    presentations, 24

Value
  creating in negotiation,
    75-76
  selling over cost, 48-49
Visual aids, presentations, 24-
    25, 33
Volunteering, benefits of,
    126-127

Waiter strategy, closing, 63
Wish list, of client, 10
Work history, of customer, 3